To Julie Tillman

Congratulations on your graduation! May you know much success and happiness, always blessed by the Lord!

THE WISE WOMAN KNOWS

Your (great - not an ajective)
Aunt Bessie Patterson

THE WISE WOMAN KNOWS

Bessie Patterson

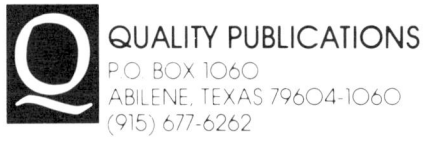
QUALITY PUBLICATIONS
P.O. BOX 1060
ABILENE, TEXAS 79604-1060
(915) 677-6262

© **Bessie Patterson** 1982

All rights reserved. No part of this publication may be reproduced, stored in a retrieval system, or transmitted in any form by any means electronic, mechanical, photocopy, recording, or otherwise, without prior permission of the copyright owner.

ISBN: 0-89137-422-1

TABLE OF CONTENTS

Table of Contents V
Dedication VI
Credits VII
Prologue 1
Chapter 1 The Wise Woman
          KNOWS 3
Chapter 2 The Wise Woman Knows
          HER HEAVENLY FATHER 11
Chapter 3 The Wise Woman Knows
          HER LORD 21
Chapter 4 The Wise Woman Knows
          THE COMFORTER 31
Chapter 5 The Wise Woman Knows
          HERSELF 41
Chapter 6 The Wise Woman Knows
          HER ROLE 51
Chapter 7 The Wise Woman Knows
          HER OPPORTUNITIES 63
Chapter 8 The Wise Woman Knows
          FREEDOM 73
Chapter 9 The Wise Woman Knows
          HAPPINESS 83
Chapter 10 The Wise Woman Knows
          PEACE 95
Chapter 11 The Wise Woman Knows
          CONTENTMENT 105
Chapter 12 The Wise Woman Knows
          HER WAY 115
Chapter 13 The Wise Woman Knows
          HER DESTINATION 123
Epilogue 134
Bibliography 135

DEDICATION

To each of YOU who, through this study, is led to a deeper commitment to Christ, that together we may render praise and glory to God . . . and with love and appreciation to my husband, Elmer Patterson, in celebration of our Golden Wedding Anniversary, June 7, 1981.

CREDITS

Scripture quotations from the NEW AMERCIAN STANDARD BIBLE, C The Lockman Foundation 1960, 1962, 1963, 1971, 1972, 1973, 1975.

Scripture quotations from the REVISED STANDARD VERSION of the Bible, by permission of the National Council of the Churches of the Churches of Christ, Division of Education and Ministry, copyrighted 1946, 1952 C 1971, 1973.

Scripture quotations from THE NEW ENGLISH BIBLE, C The Delegates of the Oxford University Press and Syndics of the Cambridge University Press 1961, 1970, reprinted by permission.

Scripture quotations from *Holy Bible: New International Version* Copyright C 1978 by the New York International Bible Society, used by permission of Zondervan Bible Publishers.

From ENCYCLOPEDIA OF WIT, HUMOR, AND WISDOM by Leewin B. Williams. Copyright renewal 1976 by Chester M. Williams. Used by permission of publisher, Abingdon Press.

From *The Christian Graces,* James M. Tolle, C Tolle Publication.

To the above I express my sincere appreciation for their permission to use the quotations in this work.

PROLOGUE

Since wisdom may be defined as the proper use of knowledge, the two actually are separate but inseparable. To be wise, there are certain things you must know. Spiritually, a knowledge of the word of God is the basis for our knowing him and being acceptable in his sight.

As usual, I am encouraging you to study the Bible, not just about the Bible. Therefore, I continue to quote passages from the scriptures to facilitate our studying them together. Obviously it has been impossible to use every scripture pertaining to each subject; so I encourage you to use your own Bible helps to delve more deeply into the truth. It will surprise you how your own interest will grow as you make a sincere effort to deepen your knowledge and understanding. I have listed daily Bible readings at the end of each chapter. They will encourage your studying these lessons daily in case you are preparing for a weekly class. Meditation in this way, from day to day, will enliven and enrich your life. And please do study the memory verses daily; make them your own; have them readily available in the wonderful "computer" of your mind. They are good mental companions when you are having to sit and wait, when you can't sleep at night, even in the dentist's chair! To help you in memorizing, write each passage on an index card which you can stand in a convenient place so that your mind may be occupied with study while your hands are busy at routine work. You *can* memorize. You will be glad you did.

"If then you are risen with Christ, seek those things which are above, where Christ is, seated at the right hand of God," a lovely silver haired octogenarian quoted happily as I met her in the aisle when she visited the local congregation recently following a year's residence in the home of her daughter. After completing her quotation of Colossians 3:1-4, she concluded, "I'll never be able to thank you enough for encouraging me to memorize that passage. It has meant so much to me!" She had observed her eightieth birthday before doing her memory work. *If she can, you can!*

I must disclaim complete originality in this effort. My life continues to be enriched by Bible classes, literature, and personal contact with others. I am deeply appreciative of all who have shared information and inspiration. For fear of omitting even one, I refrain from naming individuals, but I am thankful to each of you and to our God, to Jesus Christ, and to the Holy Spirit that whatever talent I have been given and allowed to develop may be used to His glory.

May each of you be blessed as you study individually or in class, and may the conclusion of this book find you nearer your goal of spiritual maturity than you were when you began.

In Christian love,
Bessie (Mrs. Elmer) Patterson.

Chapter 1

The Wise Woman
Knows

"Ignorance is the curse of God; knowledge the wing wherewith to fly to heaven."--Shakespeare.

As with many man-made proverbs, the above is true to a point. *What* we know and apply to our lives certainly will determine whether those wings take us upward to heaven or downward to destruction.

To know is a basic instinct. Watch a child. See it feel then taste an object. It is seeking to know. However, the instinct alone is not sufficient to ensure that the child will benefit from that knowledge. He may enjoy the taste of luscious fruit and grow physically from its contribution to his health. He may imbibe pleasant looking liquid he finds under the sink, not knowing it is furniture polish and can injure or even kill him. Even when he is older, he may know how to ride a bicycle but lack the experience to watch for cars when riding in the street. Or he may know how to drive a car just as well as does his mother, but he may not be fully aware of the danger of drag racing as he partakes avidly of its thrill of power and temporary achievement. He lacks wisdom.

"Knowledge and good judgment based on experience," is the first dictionary definition of wisdom. It continues, "Having or showing knowledge and good judgment," as the definition of *wise*. Knowledge, then, is a necessary ingredient of wisdom. However, the acquisition of good judgment through experience makes a wise woman. Someone has said that wisdom is the proper use of knowledge. That is why God ordained that children be nurtured by responsible parents until they, in turn, acquire the judgment to use their knowledge in an independent life, to make decisions for themselves which will be beneficial to them and to society.

Americans spend millions of dollars on public education; we want our children to learn, to know. Most churches spend freely for literature and teaching aids. We see the value in providing for our children the tools of learning so they may develop physically and spiritually.

The present generation has seen a veritable explosion of knowledge, especially in the scientific realm. The development of computer programs has made it possible to store and disseminate this knowledge to an extent that literally is mind-boggling. Books still flood the market, despite the prediction that television would put an end to reading. From the bulging shelves of the Library of Congress to city and county libraries flow reams of information in books, magazines, films, and tapes.

In the past 50 years we have seen an increasing development in continuing education, recognizing that one may, yea must, continue to learn or stagnate. Lest we be smothered with trivia or led astray by the wrong kind of knowledge, it is imperative that we decide *who we are* and *what* we want to know. Then we must devote ourselves to that endeavor.

Solomon's warning is doubly applicable today: "The sayings of the wise are like goads, and like nails firmly fixed are the collected sayings which are given by one Shepherd. My son, beware of anything beyond these. Of making many books there is no end, and much study is a weariness of the flesh" (Ecclesiastes 12:11,12 RSV).

I. WHY, THEN, SHOULD WE SEEK KNOWLEDGE? Why spend the time and energy, sometimes the expense, endure the "weariness of the flesh" in our quest for knowledge? Simply stated we need to know the sayings of the wise as goads to a better life. Especially in the spiritual realm, we need the "nails firmly fixed" to which we can anchor ourselves when beset by the storms of life.

A. A lack of knowledge can be dangerous. We have commented that a child may be damaged by his lack of knowledge of everyday dangers. We all have heard that lack of knowledge of the law is no excuse, but we face situations daily in which we may encounter difficulty because we did not take the time or trouble to learn the laws governing our proposed actions. A young homemaker who is also a lawyer told me that she and her husband ran into a minor hassle because they did not consult the local building code before doing some remodeling on their home.

Through the prophet Jeremiah, God warned:

"My people are fools; they do not know me.
They are senseless children; they have no understanding.
They are skilled in doing evil; they know not how to do good" (Jeremiah 4:22 NIV).

B. Spiritual ignorance may cause us to lose our souls, although we may be acting in all good conscience, with earnestness and zeal. We may wonder why the Israelites continued to transgress God's laws when He had spoken to them and their fathers directly. We forget the lapse of time covered in many instances. Generations arose who had not been taught; therefore they fell into idolatry with their heathen neighbors. Again and again God, in his mercy, sent prophets to warn them. Hosea pleaded with God's chosen people: "Listen to the word of the Lord.". . .

"My people are destroyed for lack of knowledge.
Because you have rejected knowledge,
I will reject you from being My priest.
Since you have forgotten the law of your God,
I also will forget your children" (Hosea 4:6 NASV).

Actually, there is less excuse for ignorance in this day and time, for we have the written word of God. Either indifference or prejudice can blind us to the truth; we fail to read or we do not believe to the extent of obedience. We can be like the Gentiles who were "darkened in their understanding, alienated from the life of God because of ignorance that is in them due to their hardness of heart" (Ephesians 4:18).

C. The Apostle Paul realized the value of knowledge in Christian growth. He prayed for both the Colossian and Philippian Christians to be "filled with the knowledge of his will in all wisdom and spiritual understanding," walking in a manner worthy of the Lord, being fully pleasing to him, bearing fruit in every good work, and increasing in the knowledge of God (Colossians 1:9,10; Philippians 1:9).

True knowledge of God will lead to a life of happy Christian service. As we grow in knowledge, we will grow in service. After washing the apostles' feet, stressing his teaching that his ministry was not one of pomp but of meeting the needs of others, Jesus said, "If ye know these things, happy are ye if ye do them" (Jno. 13:17, KJ).

D. Thus, our knowledge of God grows into wisdom that is truly rewarding. At times we may wonder why stories of the extreme wickedness of some men in Biblical times were recorded through inspiration. The Genesis account of Lot's plight in Sodom and Gomorrah spares no words in describing the homosexuality and general immorality of the wicked fellow citizens of that good family. Margaret Smith, wife of a missionary and evangelist, commented in a ladies' class, "The study of God's word gives us reassurance in that godly people have lived among the vilest sinners and still have maintained their spirituality."

We must develop this wisdom, based on knowledge, and impart it to our children. Much assistance in this task may be gained from reading the Book of Proverbs; here is the wise man's evaluation of wisdom; and its rewards:

> "Happy is the man who finds wisdom,
>   and the man who gets understanding,
> for the gain from it is better than gain from silver
>   and its profit better than gold.
> She is more precious than jewels,
>   and nothing you desire can compare with her.
> Long life is in her right hand;
>   in her left hand are riches and honor.
> Her ways are ways of pleasantness,
>   and all her paths are peace.
> She is a tree of life to those who lay hold on her;
>   those who hold her fast are called happy.
>   . . .
> My son, keep wisdom and discretion;
>   let them not escape from your sight,
> and they will be life for your soul
>   and adornment for your neck.
> Then you will walk on your way securely
>   and your foot will not stumble.
> (Proverbs 3:13-18; 21-23, RSV)

II. WHAT SHOULD WE KNOW? We have noted that knowledge of all descriptions is readily available to the inquiring mind of today. Also, we have begun to see that true wisdom lies in seeking knowledge from above. There are so many temptations, especially for our bright young people, to fill their minds with trash. Paul prayed that the Philippians be endowed with "all discernment." This must be our prayer for ourselves and those we influence, that we may be able to devote our time and effort to that which is inspiring and upbuilding.

A. You have only to spend a few minutes at the news stand to see that it is filled with much that, to say the least, tends more to the flesh than the spirit. A flyer from a leading men's magazine (which was promptly buried deep in our trash) proclaimed that the sample copy offered free of charge would feature an article suggesting various ways of seduction! That magazine can be bought on most news stands. Most womens' magazines have at least one feature article which is sex related. I am not suggesting that we should regress to the days of sexual ignorance, but I am pleading for some discretion.

You will remember that to be discreet is to be "wisely cautious in what we say or do." If we feed our minds deliberately on that which condones, if it does not promote actively, actions which are not in keeping with scriptural morality, we may find ourselves losing the fight against fleshly desire, so aptly described by Paul in Romans 7.

A Christian author of children's books, after having three very popular books published, found her next five manuscripts rejected because she refused to write the popular trash being offered and consumed by children. The publishers explained that there was not sufficient demand for the type of youth material she wrote, the only kind she would or could write in good conscience. Parents and even grand-parents might not be out of line to read with the children their library and even school books.

B. True, there is a world of secular knowledge which will be useful to our children in our age; but we must not forget that much worldly wisdom is foolishness with God. We will spend a lesson later on the Christian's identity. Even in choosing the knowledge we wish to gain, we must remember that we are in the world but not of it.

> Don't you know that you yourselves are God's temple and that God's Spirit lives in you? If anyone destroys God's temple, God will destroy him; for God's temple is sacred, and you are that temple. Do not deceive yourselves. If any one of you thinks he is wise by the standards of this age, he should become a "fool" so that he may become wise. For the wisdom of this world is foolishness in God's sight (1 Corinthians 3:16-19 NIV).

The wise woman will be informed. Even after marriage and motherhood, she may decide to pursue a study which was interrupted, or a taste she has developed as she matured. Community colleges, universities, and even public schools offer formal courses which may be taken for credit or audited. In addition to these, there are public service programs, all types of materials offered in public libraries, books and magazines on almost any area of study we wish to pursue.

Nothing will take the place of personal effort in acquiring the Biblical knowledge we must have to become spiritually mature. The wise woman will read her Bible from cover to cover. Thus, when someone offers her teaching not in harmony with the word, she will know it is not from God but from man. Motivation for deep study should come from Bible classes and from reading of books and magazines on related subjects. Workshops, seminars, retreats, and many activities within the fellowship of the church can inspire personal study and growth. Several new periodicals aimed at providing spiritual food for the entire family are now available.

III. KNOWLEDGE MUST BE SOUGHT AND USED FOR THE RIGHT PURPOSE. An actor may memorize the words of Moses or Christ in order to play a role he has been assigned. A Christian may actually study in order to win an argument. A student may read the Bible daily in order to receive a star or to be counted among the daily Bible readers. The wise woman is like the Jews at Berea who were called noble because they "received the word with all eagerness, examining the scriptures daily to see if these things were so" (Acts 17:11 RSV).

A. It was a desire for knowledge forbidden by God which proved the overpowering temptation for Eve. Satan lied to her; she believed his lie that she would not die if she partook of the forbidden fruit. He assured her that she would acquire knowledge of good and evil. . .that she would be like God. She rationalized that the fruit was "good for food, pleasing to the eye, and also desirable for gaining wisdom." She ate. She gave to Adam; he ate. Sin entered into the world. (Genesis 3:4-6).

Being a "know-it-all" in order to make ourselves look important is not really God-like and may actually betray our ignorance. The wise woman is aware that, regardless of how much she knows, there still is much that she has to learn. Truth presented in love builds up. Our love for God and His word will make us receptive to His teaching, put us into the proper relationship to Him.

Now about food sacrificed to idols: We know that we all possess knowledge. Knowledge puffs up, but love builds up. The man who thinks he knows something does not yet know as he ought to know. But the man who loves God is known by God (1 Corinthians 8:1-3 NIV).

B. The woman who does her daily Bible reading primarily to be able to hold up her hand when a count of readers is taken in class is not to be frowned upon because she probably will grow in her appreciation of the word and will find herself reading and studying, hungering and thirsting after righteousness. Though her motivation may have been wrong in the beginning, as she grows spiritually, her love for the Lord will grow. She will be ready to partake of the meat of the word. She will add to her knowledge both wisdom and understanding.

Make your ear attentive to wisdom,
  Incline your heart to understanding;
For if you cry for discernment,
Lift your voice for understanding;
If you seek her as silver,
And search for her as for hidden treasures;
Then you will discern the fear of the Lord,
And discover the knowledge of God.
For the Lord gives wisdom;
From His mouth come knowledge and understanding.
He stores up sound wisdom for the upright;
He is a shield to those who walk in integrity,
Guarding the paths of justice,
And He preserves the way of His godly ones.
Then you will discern righteousness and justice
And equity and every good course.
For wisdom will enter your heart,
And knowledge will be pleasant to your soul;
Discretion will guard you,
Understanding will watch over you (Proverbs 2:2-11, NASV).

Like the widow who is "dead while she lives" because of her carnal life (1 Timothy 5:6) is the woman who fails to learn the teachings of Jesus Christ, as revealed in the gospels. To know Christ really is to live.

> It is the Spirit who gives life; the flesh profits nothing; the words that I have spoken to you are spirit and are life. . . .Simon Peter answered Him, "Lord, to whom shall we go? You have words of eternal life (Jno. 6:63,68 NASV).

IV. WE REALLY LIVE WHEN HIS WORDS ARE APPLIED. It is entirely possible for one to know what she should do and still remain in sin. Many times, when counseling with negligent Christians, my husband and I have been told, "I know what I ought to do." At times I had the feeling that our presence caused them discomfort, a pricking of the conscience. Yet for some reason they were not ready to do what should be done. Sadly we have quoted James 4:17 to some who just would not obey: "Whoever knows what is right to do and fails to do it, for him it is sin" (RSV).

Knowledge of Christ through His word will set us free from evil. We can be freed from lives of indecision and doubt, for we then know whom we have believed and that he is able to guard and keep us. Knowing we are right, we will have peace of mind. Jesus said:

> If you continue in my word, you are truly my disciples, and you will know the truth, and the truth will make you free. ...Truly, truly, I say to you, every one who commits sin is a slave to sin. The slave does not continue in the house for ever; the son continues for ever. So if the Son makes you free, you will be free indeed (John 8:31,32,34-36 RSV).

CONCLUSION: The foolish woman may be ignorant because of indifference or prejudice; she may not seek truth. She may know what is right and fail to do right. She remains foolish.

The wise woman seeks knowledge of the right kind, from the right source, for the right purpose. Then she wisely applies that knowledge to a confident Christian life. She is ever mindful that "The mind of the intelligent seeks knowledge, But the mouth of fools feeds on folly." (Proverbs 15:14 NASV).

DAILY BIBLE READINGS:

Sunday: Be attentive; gain insight, Proverbs 4:1-27
Monday: Do you not know? 1 Corinthians 6:1-20
Tuesday: May we know, Acts 17:16-33
Wedneseday: Words of spirit and life, John 6:35-63
Thursday: You can not bear to hear my word. John 8:31-47
Friday: We know the spirit of truth. 1 John 4:1-6
Saturday: Taught by the spirit, 1 Corinthians 2:1-16
MEMORY VERSES: Hosea 4:6; John 8:31,32

Chapter 2

The Wise Woman Knows
HER HEAVENLY FATHER

To attempt to KNOW the Supreme Being, GOD, may appear to be presumptous on the part of a human being. Wise and inspired men have pondered the knowledge of God. They have been humbled, searching, wondering. I join them in those feelings; to me, this is the most awesome task I have attempted in these series of lessons. Yet, how can we address Him as "Our Heavenly Father" if we do not know him in a fatherly relationship? Like the men of old, we must search for Him through his revelation to us, through the things he has created, and above all, through his word. We can know Him through the eye of faith. Please join me in praying that each of us can approach this subject with purity of heart that we may claim the promise that we may see God (Matthew 5:8).

I. WE MUST ACCEPT THE FACT THAT OUR KNOWLEDGE OF GOD IS LIMITED. Surely we are not wiser or in closer relationship with God than were Job and his friends, or David, Solomon, and Paul. Their delving into the mysteries of God led them to conclude that he is unsearchable, unknown. Yet in their reverent conclusions they pointed to the WAY through which they and we could know Him.

A. Zophar voices universal questions in his attempt to convince Job that in his own life were the answers to his suffering:

Can you fathom the mysteries of God?
Can you probe the limits of the Almighty?
They are higher than the heavens--what can you do?
They are deeper than the depths of the grave--what can you know?
Their measure is longer than the earth and wider than the sea.
(Job 11:7-9 NIV)

Job was still seeking answers when he recounted the wonderful works of God in creating and maintaining the earth:

> He stretches out the north over empty space,
> And hangs the earth on nothing,
> He wraps up the waters in His clouds;
> And the cloud does not burst under them.
> He obscures the face of the full moon,
> And spreads His cloud over it.
> He has inscribed a circle on the surface of the waters,
> At the boundary of light and darkness.
> The pillars of heaven tremble,
> And are amazed at His rebuke.
> He quieted the sea with His power,
> And by His understanding He shattered Rehab.
> By His breath the heavens are cleared;
> His hand has pierced the fleeing serpent.
> Behold, these are the fringes of His ways;
> And how faint a word we hear of Him!
> But His mighty thunder, who can understand?
> (Job 26:7-14 NASV).

Not from his presumptous friends did Job receive the answers. God, himself, brought Job to his knees.

"Who is this that darkens my counsel with words without knowledge?" He asked. "Where were you when I laid the earth's foundation? Tell me, if you understand. Who marked off its dimensions? Surely you know!" (Job 38:2,4,5 NIV).

After listening to the Creator's recounting of the mighty works of creation, a pentitent Job really came to a deeper understanding of the omnipotence of God:

> Then Job replied to the Lord: "I know that you can do all things; no plan of yours can be thwarted.
> You asked, 'Who is this that obscures my counsel without knowledge?'
> Surely I spoke of things I did not understand, things too wonderful for me to know.
> "You said, 'Listen now, and I will speak; I will question you, and you shall answer me.'
> My ears had heard of you but now my eyes have seen you.
> Therefore I despise myself and repent in dust and ashes.
> (Job 42:1-6 NIV).

B. Among the many psalms extolling the God of heaven, expressed by David, is Psalm 40, in which he, too, realizes that it is impossible to bring all of God's marvels into the scope of man's understanding or counting: "Many, O Lord my God, are thy wonderful works which thou hast done, and thy thought which are to usward: they cannot be reckoned up in order unto thee: if I would declare and speak of them, they are more than can be numbered" (Psalms 40:5 KJ).

In still another psalm, David declared, "Great is the Lord, and greatly to be praised; and his greatness is unsearchable" (Psalm 145:3).

C. In his pensive, older years, the wise man, Solomon, realized that it is not in man to understand all of God's wonders, yet he recognizes that God has made known to man those things essential to his well being:

> I have seen the business that God has given to the sons of men to be busy with. He has made everything beautiful in its time; also he has put eternity into man's mind, yet so that he cannot find out what God has done from the beginning to the end. I know that there is nothing better for them than to be happy and enjoy themselves as long as they live; also that it is God's gift to man that every one should eat and drink and take pleasure in all his toil (Ecclesiastes 3:10-13 RSV).

We know that Solomon revered the Lord, yet he did not claim to understand all the wonders He had done in the earth, although Israel's third king still is called the wisest man who ever lived. In spite of his deductive reasoning he concluded:

> When I applied my mind to know wisdom and to observe man's labor on earth--his eyes not seeing sleep day or night--then I saw all that God had done. No one can comprehend what goes on under the sun. Despite all his efforts to search it out, man cannot discover its meaning. Even if a wise man claims he knows, he cannot really comprehend it (Ecclesiastes 8:16-17 NIV).

D. In writing to the Romans of God's provision of salvation for both Jew and Gentile, the apostle Paul exclaimed: "O the depth of the riches both of the wisdom and knowledge of God! how unsearchable are his judgments, and his ways past finding out!" (Romans 11:33 KJ)

In other scriptures, though, Paul makes it quite clear that God has revealed to man all that is necessary for him to know. For this reason our God is displeased with us today, as He was with the Romans, when we serve "created things rather than the Creator":

> For the wrath of God is revealed from heaven against all ungodliness and wickedness of men who by their wickedness suppress the truth. For what can be known about God is plain to them, because God has shown it to them. Ever since the creation of the world his invisible nature, namely, his eternal power and deity, has been clearly perceived in the things that have been made (Romans 1:18-20 RSV).

To the Corinthians Paul wrote of the "wisdom that has been hidden." He quoted from Isaiah 64:4, concluding that those things not previously seen had been revealed through Christ:

> "Things which eye has not seen and ear has not heard,
> and which have not entered the heart of man,
> all that God has prepared for those who love Him."
> For to us God revealed them through the Spirit; for the
> Spirit searches all things, even the depths of God...
> For, "Who has known the mind of the Lord, that he
> should instruct Him? But we have the mind of Christ.
> (1 Corinthians 2:9-10,16 NASV).

II. OUR GOD WANTS US TO KNOW HIM, TO BELIEVE IN HIM. He was always willing to reveal himself to the man who was ready to listen. In the beginning, he spoke to Adam directly; he spoke to Moses from a burning bush and from Sinai; his messages were communicated to the people through prophets. The writer of the Hebrew letter said that God spoke to the fathers in many and various ways, but in these last days he has spoken to us by His Son (Hebrews 1:1). What is important to us is not *how* we know Him, but *that* we know him:

> Thus says the Lord, "Let not a wise man boast of his wisdom, and let not the mighty man boast of his might, let not a rich man boast of his riches; but let him who boasts boast of this, that he understands and knows Me, that I am the Lord who exercises lovingkindness, justice, and righteousness on earth; for I delight in these things" (Jeremiah 9:23-24 NASV).

Moses asked, at the burning bush, what he should say to the people if they asked who had sent him.

God said to Moses, "I AM WHO I AM." and he said, "Say this to the people in Israel, 'I AM has sent me to you' " (Exodus 3:14).

"In the beginning, GOD!" He did not attempt to explain his origin; he existed and acted in the beginning. God IS. We are to accept that fact and to know him as he reveals himself to us...through his word.

Later, in Exodus 6:2, he explained to Moses: "I am the Lord. I appeared to Abraham, to Isaac and to Jacob as God Almighty, but by my name the Lord I did not make myself known to them."

The American Standard version renders the above name as *"Jehova"*. In the column note, the New American Standard explains that the name in the original is YHWH*, usually translated *"Lord"*. It is interesting to note that Moffatt used *the "Eternal"*, in this passage.

It appears that, regardless of the name by which he has been called, we can come to know, revere, and serve him as *Lord*.

III. OUR REVERENCE FOR THE ETERNAL DEEPENS AS WE REALIZE HIS CHARACTERISTICS. We must realize that he is a spiritual being, that he can not be defined in human terms, identified by appearance as a person is known. In awe, Solomon exclaimed in his dedication of the temple, "Heaven and the heaven of heavens cannot contain thee!" (1 Kings 8:27).

He is omnipresent, omnicient, omnipotent, immutable, just, and holy.

A. A mother was explaining God's omnipresence to her little son. "You mean God is everywhere, all at once?" the wondering child asked.

Receiving an affirmative answer, he continued, "You mean he is in this house? in this room?"

"Yes, he's everywhere," the mother affirmed.

"In that sugar bowl?"

The mother thought that was going a bit far but she had to agree.

"Oh, boy! Got him!" the boy chortled as he slapped his hand over the sugar bowl.

Sometimes we may be as naive in our attempts to contain God in cultural or religious barriers. What a wonderful thought. Our God is not limited; he can not be contained even in the heaven of heavens. much less the earthly temple built by Solomon. Yet "he is not far from each one of us." (Acts 17:27).

His presence everywhere can be a comfort to the lonely; it is pleasant to those who love him and are in covenant relationship with him. It can help each of us to walk circumspectly. No one else may see what we are doing, but God sees and knows...even when we are on vacation, away from those for whom we must set a good example.

B. Not only does God see everything, because he is everywhere, but he also knows everything. He is omnicient. He knows our needs before we express them to him in prayer, yet we are told to let our requests be made known to God by prayer and supplication, with thanksgiving. (Philippians 4:6). Others may have false impressions of us, may even lie about us. But God knows and cares. We may be able to fool others, but God knows what we do, even what we think. This is not to picture him as one spying on us, looking for something wrong. Peter says, "He cares about you." (1 Peter 5:6).

This then is how we know that we belong to the truth, and how we set our hearts at rest in his presence whenever our hearts condemn us. For God is greater than our hearts, and he knows everything. (1 John 3:19,20 NIV).

C. God is omnipotent. "Mightier than the thunders of many waters, mightier than the waves of the sea, the Lord on high is mighty!" (Psalms 93:4). God spoke the world into existence. Through the power of his word, he set it in order. Throughout the first chapter of Genesis, we read: "God, said...and it was so." Oh, that we might comprehend and believe God's power! There was no doubt in the minds of Shadrach, Meshach, and Abednego when they faced the alternative of worshiping an idol or being cast into a fiery furnace. They declared, "Our God whom we serve is able to deliver us from the burning fiery furnace; and he will deliver us out of your hand, O king." (Daniel 3:17, RSV).

"With God all things are possible," Jesus declared. (Matthew 19:26). He reminded the Pharisees, who boasted that they were children of Abraham, that God is able to raise up children of Abraham from stones. It was God's power that raised Jesus from the dead. Paul prayed that the Ephesians might know God's incomparably great power for believers, identifying it as that used by God in the resurrection of Christ (Ephesians 1:19,20).

D. God is immutable; that is, he does not change. "I am the Lord, I change not," was God's declaration through Malachi (Malachi 3:6). We live in a world of change. It is true that some change is good; our health improves; we achieve financial gain, are able to take advantage of opportunities for self improvement, to raise our standard of living. Yet we and our children may feel we live on the shifting sand as we see society accepting "life sytles" in contrast to our moral standards which we have derived from God's word. We turn to our unchanging God for reassurance, thankful that there is a rock to which we can cling. Despite anything the world may say, we must not let ourselves be deceived. We know that "Every good and perfect gift is from above, coming down from the Father of the heavenly lights, who does not change like shifting shadows" (James 1:17 NIV).

---

*Editor's note: YHWH is probably better rendered *Yahweh.*

E. Our God is just, true, holy, righteous. Since he is the embodiment of all that is good, the list might go on and on. Some say they can not believe in a God who would send a man to a burning hell. They fail to realize that it is not God, but sin, which dooms a man. Since God is just and holy, he can not condone sin; he offers a way of salvation to every man. He is just and allows each responsible individual to accept or reject the way of escape. Those who overcome will sing with the redeemed:

"Great and marvelous are your deeds,
  Lord God Almighty.
Just and true are your ways,
  King of the ages.
Who will not fear you, O Lord,
  and bring glory to your name?
For you alone are holy.
All nations will come
  and worship before you,
for your righteous acts have been revealed. (Rev.15:3-4 NIV)

F. God is love. John 3:16 is justifiably called the golden text of the Bible, for it tells of a love so great that it prompted the gift of God's only begotten son so that those who believe on him may have eternal life. Just as other attributes of God are almost beyond our comprehension, so is his love. Do you have a son? Would you give your son that a sinner, perhaps one who had wronged you, could be saved? See what I mean? But that is exactly what God did, what he is. We must remember, though, that our loving God is also a just God, a holy God who can not condone sin.

John describes God's love and our response to that love so beautifully:

Beloved, let us love one another; for love is of God and he who loves is born of God and knows God. He who does not love does not know God; for God is love. In this the love of God was made manifest among us, that God sent his only Son into the world, so that we might live through him...By this we know that we love the children of God, when we love God and obey his commandments. For this is the love of God that we keep his commandments. And his commandments are not burdensome (1 John 4:7-9; 5:2-3 RSV).

IV. TO HIM BE THE GLORY. How can the created glorify the creator? Realizing his awesome greatness, we recognize our total inadequacy in his presence. Yet, in his great love, he has provided an avenue through which, or perhaps I should say, through whom we can approach him. Jesus said, "I am the way, and the truth, and the life; no one comes to the Father, but by me" (John 14:6 RSV).

A. We are to love God. Jesus cited this as the most important command: "Love the Lord your God with all your heart and with all your soul and with all your mind and with all your strength" (Mark 12:30 NIV). This is a love which involves our total being, our intellect, our will, our emotion, to the extent that we will employ every fibre of our strength to his glory and praise. This is a love which will prompt us to obey the commandments of God. Remember, "This is the love of God, that we keep his commandments" (1 John 5:3).

B. We count it a privilege, not a duty, to worship our heavenly father. In his conversation with the Samaritan woman, Jesus said,"The hour is coming, and now is, when true worshipers will worship the Father in spirit and truth, for such the Father seeks to worship him" (John 4:23). We might describe this as heart-felt religion or worship; it is not cold and ritualistic, but warm and loving. Yet we do recognize that our worship can be vain if it is based on the commandments of men; so we must follow the avenues of worship provided in his word. We must worship in truth, alone or when we assemble with the saints.

We will offer whole hearted worship, following Paul's admonition: "Therefore, I urge you, brothers, in view of God's mercy, to offer your bodies as living sacrifices, holy and pleasing to God--which is your spiritual worship" (Romans 12:1 NIV).

CONCLUSION: Because of her errant ways, the foolish woman will face the severity of God; the wise woman will know his goodness:

Behold therefore the goodness and severity of God: on them which fell, severity; but toward thee, goodness, if thou continue in his goodness (Romans 11:22 KJ).

Realizing God's greatness and majesty, the wise woman is overcome with reverence and awe. Her love and obedience are prompted by God's great, redemptive love. With Paul she exclaims:

Oh, the depth of the riches of the wisdom and knowledge of God!
How unsearchable his judgments, and his paths beyond tracing out!
Who has known the mind of the Lord?
For from him and through him and to him are all things.
To him be the glory forever! Amen (Romans 11:33-36 RSV).

DAILY BIBLE READINGS:

Sunday: Can you find the limit of the Almighty? Job 11:1-20
Monday: God, my refuge, Psalms 71:1-21
Tuesday: Will you put God in the wrong? Job 40:1-14
Wednesday: God put eternity in man's mind. Ecclesiastes 3:1-15
Thursday: A living sacrifice, Romans 12:1-21
Friday: The living God, 1 John 5:1-12
Saturday: The conclusion, Ecclesiastes 12:1-14

MEMORY VERSES:

Jeremiah 9:23,24
1 John 4:7-9

Chapter 3

The Wise Woman Knows
HER LORD

We hear much today about knowing Jesus. This is good if one is an informed seeker, if she seeks him through God's word, the only source of divine truth. While her emotion is involved as she realizes what he has done for her, she is not seeking an emotion-charged experience, per se. Some have said, "I have been a Christian for years but did not know Jesus as the Lord of my life." Apparently that statement is made by one who obeyed a form of doctrine without becoming a new person. That, literally, is what is meant by *conversion*. It is an about-face, a decision to lose self in Christ. This decision is prompted by faith in Jesus as the Christ, the Son of God. One need not be a Bible scholar, but she must have heard enough of the word to produce faith in Christ. Faith comes by hearing the word of God (Romans 10:17). John said he wrote his gospel, recording many things that Jesus did, in order that the reader might believe and have eternal life (John 20:30,31).

Since most who read or study this book will be familiar with the story of Christ's life here on earth, we will devote our attention to his relationship to God and ours to God through him as Lord. It would strengthen our faith and enrich our study if we took the time to reread at least one of the four gospels, all four if possible. In the words of Paul, my prayer for those who are studying with us is that they may have the full riches of complete understanding, in order that they may know the mystery of God, namely, Christ, in whom are hidden all the treasures of wisdom and knowledge" (Colossians 2:2b, 3, NIV).

I. JESUS CHRIST IS CO-ETERNAL WITH GOD. While we may be inclined to think of the life of Christ as only the thirty-three years he lived on the earth, like God, he is eternal. He was with God in the beginning and participated in creation:

In the beginning was the Word, and the Word was with God, and the Word was God. He was in the beginning with God; all things were made through him, and without him was not anything made that was made...And the Word became flesh and dwelt among us full of grace and truth; we have beheld his glory, glory as of the only Son from the Father (John 1:1-3, 14, RSV).

Also present and active in creation was the Spirit. We read in Genesis 1:2: "And the earth was without form, and void; and darkness was upon the face of the deep. And the Spirit of God moved upon the face of the waters." We will find later in this lesson that all three are active in our salvation.

II. HE CHOSE TO ASSUME A DIFFERENT ROLE. That one who was equal with God should choose to live in human form is almost beyond the grasp of our finite minds. He was unlimited by time or space, yet he chose to assume the limitations of a body of flesh and blood. In writing to the Philippians, Paul cites Christ's example as the epitome of humility:

Your attitude should be the same as that of Christ Jesus:
Who, being in very nature God, did not consider equality
    with God something to be grasped,
but made himself nothing, taking the very nature of a servant,
    being made in human likeness.
And being found in appearance as a man,
    he humbled himself and became obedient to death--
    even death on a cross!
Therefore God exalted him to the highest place
    and gave him the name that is above every name,
that at the name of Jesus every knee should bow,
    in heaven and on earth and under the earth,
and every tongue confess that Jesus Christ is Lord,
    to the glory of God the Father. (Philippians 2:5-11, NIV)

Not only did he come as a human being, he was born, in fulfillment of prophecy, to a virgin. He did not come in royal splendor but was wrapped in swaddling clothes and laid in a manger because there was no room for them in the inn (Luke 2:7). This, too, was in fulfillment of prophecy, as was his birth in Bethlehem. After the visit of the wise men, Joseph obeyed God's instruction to take Mary and the Baby Jesus to Egypt, where they stayed until after Herod's death, thus escaping the wicked king's slaughter of all male children under two years of age. On their return, when God directed, they live in Nazareth, thus fulfilling the prophecy that he would be called a Nazarene.

A. The scriptures are silent on Jesus' early childhood; we do know that he had brothers and sisters (Matthew 13:55,56). It is safe to assume that he lived the normal life of a Jewish boy, playing with his siblings, being taught by his parents. His body was that of a normal boy; when he stubbed his bare toe, it bled and hurt, just as that of any little boy.

Luke does record the story of his going with his parents to Jerusalem when he was twelve years old. This is the first indication we have that he was, as a child, aware of his divine nature. He stayed behind in Jerusalem. After traveling a day's journey, supposing he was in the company of kinsfolk, his parents realized he was missing and returned to look for him. Someone has siad that they looked in all the wrong places first, for they found him in the temple on the third day. He was sitting among the teachers; everyone who heard him was amazed at his understanding and his answers.

His parents also were astonished; "Son, why have you treated us so? Behold, your father and I have been looking for you anxiously," his mother said.

"How is it that you sought me? Did you not know that I must be in my Father's house?" he replied.

He returned with them to Nazareth and was obedient to them. He set an example, even then, that can be followed by every boy and girl. He grew in"wisdom and stature, and in favor with God and man" (Luke 2:41-52). His was a well-rounded development. He was learning and growing; apparently his parents were careful to see that his body was nourished properly and given exercise, some of which probably was in working with his earthly father in his carpenter shop. He learned to get along with those of his household and with their associates. He was taught God's will, was an obedient child. He grew mentally, physically, socially, and spiritually.

Mary had been told, "The Holy Spirit will come upon you, and the power of the Most High will overshadow you; therefore the child to be born will be called holy, the Son of God" (Luke 2:35 RSV).

B. John had begun his ministry, crying, "Prepare the way for the Lord." We next hear of Jesus, after a lapse in chronology of 18 years, when he came to John to be baptized. When Jesus came up from the water of baptism, the heavens were opened, and he saw the Spirit of God descending like a dove, and alighting on him, and a voice from heaven said, "This is my beloved Son, with whom I am well pleased" (Matthew 3:13-17).

Luke tells us that Jesus was about 30 years of age when he began his ministry. After his temptation in the wilderness, when he resisted Satan's mightiest efforts with a confident "It is written," he plunged into a tireless ministry which lasted some three years. He spent his time teaching, healing, training his apostles, proving that he truly was the Son of God. When John the Baptist was in prison, he apparently wanted to confirm his teaching about the Christ; he had his disciples ask, "Are you he who is to come, or shall we look for another?"

Jesus answered: "Go tell John what you hear and see: the blind receive their sight and the lame walk, lepers are cleansed and the deaf hear, and the dead are raised up, and the poor have good news preached to them" (Matthew 11:2-5 RSV).

C. On various occasions Jesus testified that he is the Son of God. When the Jews challenged him, he replied, "Do you say of him whom the Father consecrated and sent into the world, 'You are blaspheming,' because I said, 'I am the Son of God'? If I am not doing the works of my Father, then do not believe me; but if I do them, even though you do not believe me, believe the works, that you may know and understand that the Father is in me and I am in the Father" (John 10:36-38 RSV).

"Who do you say I am?" Jesus asked his disciples.

Simon Peter answered, "You are the Christ, the Son of the living God." Jesus then revealed that on this truth he would build his church (Matthew 16:15-18 NIV).

As Jesus was approaching the climax of his life on earth, God again expressed his approval and indicated that Jesus was to supercede both Moses and the prophets. He took with him Peter, James, and John to a high mountain where he was transfigured. Luke says that Moses and Elijah appeared in glory and spoke of his departure, which he was to accomplish at Jerusalem (Luke 9:28-35).

Peter said, "Lord, it is good for us to be here. If you wish, I will put up three shelters--one for you, one for Moses and one for Elijah."

While he was still speaking, a bright cloud enveloped them, and a voice from the cloud said, "This is my Son, whom I love; with him I am well pleased. Listen to him!" (Matthes 17:4-5 NIV).

D. In presenting Jesus as the Word, in the passage quoted above, John presented him as God's means of communicating with man. It also might indicate that he is the personification of truth, for Jesus said in his prayer just before his betrayal, "Sanctify them by the truth; your word is truth" (John 17:17 NIV). He had told his apostles, "I am the way, and the truth, and the life; no one comes to the Father, but by me" (John 14:6 RSV). He continued in verse 7, "If you had known me, you would have known my Father also; henceforth you know him and have seen him."

The writer of Hebrews also makes it amply clear that it is through his Son that he speaks to those in the Christian age, that we are to hear Jesus, the Christ, the Anointed:

> In many and various ways God spoke of old to our fathers by the prophets; but in these last days he has spoken to us by a Son, whom he appointed the heir of all things, through whom also he created the world. He reflects the glory of God and bears the very stamp of his nature, upholding the universe by his word of power. When he had made purification for sins, he sat down at the right hand of Majesty on high, having become as much superior to angels as the name he has obtained is more excellent than theirs. For to what angel did God ever say,
>
> "Thou art my Son, today I have begotten thee"?
>
> (Hebrews 1:1-5 RSV).

III. GOD'S ETERNAL PURPOSE IS REALIZED IN CHRIST. After Adam and Eve had sinned and fallen, God began to reveal his purpose which would bring man back into covenant relationship with him. He promised enmity between the seed of the serpent and of the woman, saying, "He shall bruise your head, and you shall bruise his heel" (Genesis 3:15). This is seen by Bible scholars as the first prophecy of the coming of Christ as the *seed* of woman.

Abraham was promised that in him and his *seed* all nations would be blessed (Genesis 13:15,16). Paul comments on this passage, showing that it is a prophecy of the coming of Christ, "The promises were spoken to Abraham and to his seed. The Scripture does not say "and to seeds," meaning many people, but "and to your seed," meaning one person, who is Christ" (Galatians 3:16 NIV).

A. God's mystery is made known in Christ. Although the prophets were used to foretell Christ's coming, they were not permitted to see their words fulfilled. Paul points out that we who live in this age are able to see what they longed to see.

> When you read this you can perceive my insight into the mystery of Christ, which was not made known to the sons of men in other generations as it has now been revealed to his holy apostles and prophets by the Spirit; that is, how the Gentiles

are fellow heirs, members of the same body, and partakers of the promise in Christ Jesus through the gospel.

Of this gospel I was made a minister according to the gift of God's grace which was given me by the working of his power. To me, though I am the very least of all the saints, this grace was given, to preach to the Gentiles the unsearchable riches of Christ, and to make all men see what is the plan of the mystery hidden for ages in God who created all things; that through the church the manifold wisdom of God might now be made known to the principalities and powers in the heavenly places. This was according to the eternal purpose which he has realized in Christ Jesus our Lord, in whom we have boldness and confidence of access through faith in him (Ephesians 3:4-12 RSV).

We see that God's plan now includes both Jew and Gentile and that it is through the church, which Jesus said he would build, that God's wisdom and his plan for man's reconciliation to him were to be revealed. Access to this blessing is to come through faith in Christ Jesus.

B. In Christ's kingdom, the church, we have redemption. There are those who say, "Jesus, 'yes' the church, 'no'." This is impossible. It is God's plan that we be redeemed in the body of Christ, which is his church, his kingdom. In writing to the Colossians, Paul makes this amply clear to any one who will accept God's word without preconceived ideas.

He has delivered us from the dominion of darkness and transferred us to the kingdom of his beloved Son, in whom we have redemption, the forgiveness of sins...He is the head of the body, the church; he is the beginning, the first-born from the dead, that in everything he might be pre-eminent. For in him all the fullness of God was pleased to dwell, and through him to reconcile to himself all things, whether on earth or in heaven, making peace by the blood of his cross. And you who were estranged and hostile in mind, doing evil deeds, he has now reconciled in his body of flesh by his death, in order to present you holy and blameless and irreproachable before him, provided that you continue in the faith, stable and steadfast, not shifting from the hope of the gospel which you heard (Colossians 1:13, 18-23 RSV).

IV. In his exaltation, Jesus was made LORD and CHRIST. Actually, Jesus is the name given by Mary and Joseph to the babe born in the manger. Christ is his title, the Anointed. Therefore, we know him as Jesus Christ. *Lord* comes from KURIOS, meaning having power or authority. Before he gave the great commission, Jesus announced that all power had been given to him, in heaven and on earth (Matthew 28:18). In concluding the first gospel sermon, recorded in Acts 2, Peter declared, "Therefore, let all Israel be assured of this: God has made this Jesus, whom you crucified, both Lord and Christ" (Acts 2:36 NIV).

A. Since he has all authority, has been made Lord by the Father, to make him our Lord we must accept his authority. He continued in Matthew 28: "Go ye therefore and teach all nations, baptizing them in the name of the Father, and of the Son, and of the Holy Ghost: Teaching them to observe all things whatsoever I have commanded you: and, lo, I am with you always, even unto the end of the world" (Matthew 28:19,20 KJ).

When the Jews who heard Peter's sermon on the day of Pentecost heard his declaration that they had killed the Son of God, the one whom God had made Lord and Christ, they asked what they must do, and Peter said to them, "Repent, and be baptized every one of you in the name of Jesus Christ for the remission of sins, and ye shall receive the gift of the Holy Ghost" (Acts 2:38 KJ).

Jesus said all nations were to be taught. Peter taught the thousands listening to the first gospel sermon. Jesus had said those who would not believe in him would die in their sins (John 8:24). John said that all believers are given power to become children of God (John 1:12). The believers who heard Peter were "pricked in their hearts," repented, and about 3,000 were baptized that day. Acts 2:47 says they were added to the church. They were reconciled to God.

B. BAPTIZED BELIEVERS ARE IN HIS BODY, THE CHURCH. There are other scriptures teaching the necessity of obeying Christ. We noted above that believers could become children of God. We read in Galatians 3:26, 27, RSV, "For in Christ Jesus you are all sons of God, through faith. For as many of you as were baptized into Christ have put on Christ."

In Ephesians 1:3 we learn that all spiritual blessings, with which God has blessed us, are in Christ. To have access to those blessings, then, we must be in Christ.

C. HE IS OUR LORD, THEN, WHEN WE ARE IN HIS BODY. We gladly confess him as Lord, both with our lips and in our lives.

Paul said, "If you confess with your lips that Jesus is Lord and believe in your heart that God raised him from the dead, you will be saved. For man believes with his heart and so is justified, and he confesses with his lips and so is saved" (Romans 10:9,10 RSV). When we claim him as Lord, we must be willing to follow him, to obey his commands. This is the way we show our love for him, for he said, "If you love me, you will keep my commandments" (John 14:15).

We show our love for him by loving one another. The old law had said that we should love our neighbor as ourself. Jesus gave a new commandment, that we love one another as he loved us (John 13:34). He gave his life that we might be redeemed from sin. We are to love with a selfless love.

He came to do his Father's will. We must walk as he walked. If we do not, it is futile for us to call him Lord. Merely calling him "Lord," without doing his will, will not save us. He said, "Not every one who says to me, 'Lord, Lord,' shall enter the kingdom of heaven, but he who does the will of my Father who is in heaven" (Matthew 7:21 RSV).

D. LEAD A LIFE WORTHY OF YOUR LORD. Paul prayed for the Colossians that they might "be filled with the knowledge of his will in all spiritual wisdom and understanding, to lead a life worthy of the Lord, fully pleasing to him, bearing fruit in every good work and increasing in the knowledge of God." This is my prayer for you.

To be filled with the knowledge of his will, you must study his word and pray for understanding. Study with an open mind, be receptive to his teaching. "As newborn babes, desire the sincere milk of the word, that ye may grow thereby" (1 Peter 2:2 KJ).

Each Christian has a vital place in the body of Christ. Each can use her own talent to the Lord's glory. This is his plan for growth of his body.

> It was he who gave some to be apostles, some to be prophets, some to be evangelists, and some to be pastors and teachers, to prepare God's people for works of service, so that the body of Christ may be built up until we all reach unity in the faith and in the knowledge of the Son of God and becomd mature, attaining to the whole measure of the fullness of Christ. Then we will no longer be infants, tossed back and forth by the waves, and blown here and there by every wind of teaching and by the cunning and craftiness of men in their deceitful scheming. Instead, speaking the truth in love, we will in all things grow up

into him who is the Head, that is, Christ. From him the whole body, joined and held together by every supporting ligament, grows and builds itself up in love, as each part does its work (Ephesians 4:11-16 NIV).

Paul's epistles are filled with teaching which will help us "build ourselves up in love." Especially in Romans 1, Colossians 3, Ephesians 4, and Galatians 5 he tells us what sin is, listing the things we are to remove from our lives. In the latter three, he also lists the fruits of the spirit and the Christ-like qualities we are to emulate.

V. KNOWING GOD AND CHRIST IS ETERNAL LIFE. As he approached his sacrificial death on the cross, he prayed for his disciples and for all who believe on him through their words. His thought was not of what he had given up, or of what he was facing. He thought and prayed about the tremendous gift awaiting the faithful.

Father, the time has come. Glorify your Son, that your Son may glorify you. For you granted him authority over all people that he might give eternal life to all those you have given him. Now this is eternal life: that they may know you, the only true God, and Jesus Christ, whom you have sent. (John 17:1-3 NIV)

In fact, he says knowing Christ and God IS eternal life. Again in his later epistle, John speaks of the testimony God has given of his Son: "God has given us eternal life, and this life is in his Son. He who has the Son has life; he who does not have the Son of God does not have life" (1 John 5:11,12 NIV).

CONCLUSION: The foolish woman makes God a liar, for she does not believe God's testimony concerning his Son. She is "dead while she lives." The wise woman believes God's testimony and can call Jesus Christ Lord because she loves him and keeps his commandments. She has eternal life in God's Son.

DAILY BIBLE READINGS:
Sunday: The crucified and risen Lord, Luke 23:1-24:50
Monday: The church established, Acts 2:1-47
Tuesday: Forgiveness for a Christian who sins, Acts 8:9-24
    A New Testament conversion, Acts 8:26-40
Wednesday: Free from sin, slaves of righteousness, Romans 6:1-23
Thursday: A life of love, hope, rejoicing, 1 Thessalonians 4:1-12
Friday: Walk by the Spirit; look to yourself, Galatians 5:16-6:18
Saturday: Walk in the light, 1 John 1:1-2:6
MEMORY VERSES: Philippians 2:5-11

Chapter 4

The Wise Woman Knows
THE COMFORTER

Because of controversy in the religious world, we often shy away from a study of the Holy Spirit. It is true that there are misconceptions and misrepresentations of his work. Is this true because we have not accepted him in faith? Through faith gained by our study of the scriptures we accept God and Christ. Those same scriptures will lead us to appreciate the Comforter, whom Jesus said the Father would send. Why can we not accept the Holy Spirit with the same trusting faith in which we receive the daily "miracles" of our lives? Can you analyze sunlight, the wind, rain clouds...the birth of a child? Does the expectant mother think she must know just how and when each tiny limb is made? Solomon expressed it this way:

"As you do not know the path of the wind,
 or how the body is formed in a mother's womb,
so you cannot understand the work of God,
  the Maker of all things." (Ecclesiastes 11:5 NIV)

I. THE HOLY SPIRIT IS A PERSONALITY. When we speak of the Spirit, we have a tendency to say *it*. He is the third person of the divine trinity, God the Father, the Son, and the Holy Spirit. Just as the Christ was with the Father in the beginning, so was the Spirit of God. He shares attributes of God and Christ.

A. He is eternal. In Genesis 1:2 we read, "And the Spirit of God moved upon the face of the waters."

That the Spirit was ever present and working with God and Christ is indicated by the writer of Hebrews: "How much more shall the blood of Christ, who through the eternal Spirit offered himself without spot to God, purge your conscience from dead works to serve the living God?" (Hebrews 9:14 KJ).

B. He is omnipresent. The psalmist said, "Whither shall I go from thy Spirit?" (Psalms 139:7). Although he came as comforter after

Jesus ascended to heaven, he is seen working actively with God, or we might say for God, in many Old Testament instances. Of Othniel, Gideon, Samson, Saul, David and others it was said, "And the Spirit of the Lord came upon him." Thus they performed mighty physical feats, were victorious in battle, uttered prophecies (Numbers 24:2; Judges 3:10; 6:34; 14:6; 1 Samuel 10:10; 16:13).

C. Like God, the Spirit is omnipotent. Job recognized him as active in his own life: "The Spirit of God has made me" (Job 33:4).

Paul spoke repeatedly of the power of the Holy Spirit. He declared that it was "in the power of the Spirit" that he preached the gospel to the Gentiles, resulting in their obedience (Romans 15:18,19).

"Now may the God of hope fill you with all joy and peace in believing, that you may abound in hope by the power of the Holy Spirit" (Romans 15:13 NASV). This was his prayer for the Roman Christians.

The Spirit was associated with power in Christ's ministry and in his promise to the apostles. After his temptation in the wilderness, Luke said, "And Jesus returned in the power of the Spirit into Galilee" (4:14). "You shall receive power when the Holy Spirit has come upon you," Jesus told the apostles just before his ascension (Acts 1:8). In the following chapter we see the demonstration of that power as Jews of every nation heard the teaching of the Spirit-endued apostles telling the gospel news, and each man heard in his own language.

D. He is omniscient. He was active, as Jesus promised he would be, in helping the writers of the New Testament to recall his teaching and to reveal the wisdom of God. Paul explained this in writing to the Corinthians:

> We speak of God's secret wisdom, a wisdom that has been hidden and that God destined for our glory before time began. None of the rulers of this age understood it, for if they had, they would not have crucified the Lord of glory. However, as it is written:
>
> > "No eye has seen,
> > no ear has heard,
> > no mind has conceived
> > what God has prepared for
> > those who love him." (Isaiah 64:4)
>
> but God has revealed it to us by his Spirit. The Spirit searches all things, even the deep things of God. For who among men

knows the thoughts of a man except the man's spirit within him? In the same way no one knows the thoughts of God except the Spirit of God. We have not received the spirit of the world but the Spirit is from God, that we may understand what God has freely given us. (1 Corinthians 2:7-12 NIV)

II. THE HOLY SPIRIT WORKS WITH THE FATHER AND SON.

In his promise of the coming comforter, Jesus indicated that he would be directed by the Father, recalling the teaching of the Christ:

When the Spirit of truth comes, he will guide you into all the truth; for he will not speak on his own authority, but whatever he hears he will speak, and he will declare to you the things that are to come. He will glorify me, for he will take what is mine and declare it to you. All that the Father has is mine; there fore I said that he will take what is mine and declare it to you (John 16:13-15 RSV).

A. He was instrumental in carrying out the will of the Father in his dealings with the Israelites. The Levites reminded them as they were preparing to return from captivity to Jerusalem that God gave his Spirit to instruct their forefathers while they were wandering in the wilderness (Nehemiah 9:20). Through an angel, Zerubbabel was told " 'Not by might nor by power, but by My Spirit,' says the Lord of hosts" (Zechariah 4:6 NASV).

B. The outpouring of the Spirit was foretold by the prophets. Speaking in symbolic language, Isaiah declared: "The fortress will be abandoned, the noisy city deserted; citadel and watchtower will become a wasteland forever, the delight of donkeys, a pasture for flocks, till the Spirit is poured upon us from on high, and the desert becomes a fertile field...Justice will dwell in the desert and righteousness live in the fertile field" (Isaiah 32:14-16 NIV).

Speaking of the return of the remnant from captivity, Ezekiel spoke for the Lord, saying, "I will no longer hide my face from them, for I will pour out my Spirit on the house of Israel" (Ezekiel 39:29 NIV).

Perhaps the most noted of these prophecies is that of Joel, cited by Peter on the Day of Pentecost: "And afterward, I will pour out my Spirit on all people. Your sons and daughters will prophesy, your old men will dream dreams, your young men will see visions. Even on my servants, both men and women, I will pour out my Spirit in those days" (Joel 2:28,29 NIV).

C. Both Jesus and the Father would be involved in the coming of the Spirit as the Comforter after Christ's ascension. He is called, also, the Counselor (RSV and NIV) and Helper (NASV). Jesus promised, "But the Comforter, even the Holy Spirit, whom the Father will send in my name, he shall teach you all things, and bring to your remembrance all that I said unto you" (John 14:26 ASV).

D. He was instrumental in the conception of the Son of God. After Gabriel had been sent by God to inform Mary that she would be the mother of his son, she asked, "How will this be, since I am a virgin?" The angel answered, "The Holy Spirit will come upon you, and the power of the Most High will overshadow you. So the holy one to be born will be called the Son of God" (Luke 1:34,35 NIV).

E. Both the Father and the Spirit manifested approval of Jesus at his baptism. We are told by Luke that the Holy Spirit in bodily form like a dove descended on him. Then the Father expressed his love and approbation of the Son (Luke 3:22).

F. Jesus included the Trinity in giving the great commission, as recorded in Mathew 28:19. Believers are to be baptized in the name of the Father and of the Son and of the Holy Spirit. This is not merely a formula to be said as one is baptized, although it is most appropriate at this solemn reinactment of the death, burial, and resurrection of the Lord. Jesus had just said that all authority in heaven and on earth had been given him, but he chose to recognize the unity of the three in this act of faith.

III. THE BAPTISM OF THE HOLY SPIRIT WAS PROMISED TO THE APOSTLES. Just before his ascension, Jesus said (through the Holy Spirit to the apostles, Acts 1:2), "Do not leave Jerusalem, but wait for the gift my Father promised, which you have heard me speak about. For John baptized with water, but in a few days you will be baptized with the Holy Spirit" (Acts 1:4b,5 NIV).

A. Between the giving of this promise and its fulfillment, the apostles had seen fit to select a man to take the place of Judas Iscariot. Apparently this was done with the guidance of the Spirit, for two men, Barsabbas and Matthias, had been nominated. After praying, they drew lots, and the lot fell on Matthias, who was then numbered with the eleven. This incident is recorded in the final verses of the first chapter of Acts. In the first verse of Acts 2 we hear that they were all together in one place. Evidently, *they* refers to the *twelve apostles.* The account of their baptism with the Holy Spirit follows:

> When the day of Pentecost had come, they were all together in one place. And suddenly a sound came from heaven like the

rush of a mighty wind, and it filled all the house where they were sitting. And there appeared to them tongues as of fire, distributed and resting on each one of them. And they were all filled with the Holy Spirit and began to speak in other tongues, as the Spirit gave them utterance (Acts 2:1-4 RSV).

B. The first Gentile converts also received the baptism of the Holy Spirit. After Peter's vision on the housetop, convincing him that God was no respecter of persons, the Spirit told him not to hesitate to go with the men sent to him by Cornelius, a devout Gentile from Caeserea, who also had had a vision and was told to send for Peter. In the mean time, Cornelius had invited his relatives and close friends to hear what Peter was instructed to tell them. The exact number is not recorded, but we are told that Peter found a large gathering of people when he entered the house.

Peter then spoke of the "good news of peace through Jesus Christ." He recounted how God had anointed Jesus of Nazareth with the Holy Spirit and power, and how he went around doing good and healing all who were under the power of the devil. He declared that he was a witness of Jesus' work and teaching, of his crucifixion and resurrection, of his appearance after he had arisen. He noted the testimony of the prophets that believers in the Christ would receive forgiveness of sins through his name. His sermon was interrupted by the coming of the Holy Spirit:

> While Peter was still speaking these words, the Holy Spirit came on all who heard the message. The circumcised believers who had come with Peter were astonished that the gift of the Holy Spirit had been poured out even on the Gentiles. For they heard them speaking in tongues and praising God (Acts 10:44-46 NIV).

One might surmise that the above was simply the gift of the Spirit promised through Peter on the Day of Pentecost to pentitent, baptized believers. This can not be true, though, for immediately following the above verses we read:

> Then Peter said, "Can anyone keep these people from being baptized with water? They have received the Holy Spirit just as we have." So he ordered that they be baptized in the name of Jesus Christ (Acts 10:47-48 NIV).

Peter further identifies the coming of the Spirit on the household of Cornelius as identical to that on Pentecost when he defended his action before criticizing believers in Jerusalem:

As I began to speak, the Holy Spirit came on them as he had come on us at the beginning. Then I remembered what the Lord had said, 'John baptized with water, but you will be baptized with the Holy Spirit.' So if God gave them the same gift as he gave us, who believed in the Lord Jesus Christ, who was I to think that I could oppose God? (Acts 11:15-17 NIV)

IV. THE GOSPEL WAS RECORDED THROUGH INSPIRATION OF THE SPIRIT. In the first of his epistles, Peter said the prophets searched and inquired about the salvation to come through Jesus Christ, saying "It was revealed to them that they were serving not themselves but you, in the things which have now been announced to you by those who preached the good news to you through the Holy Spirit sent from heaven" (1 Peter 1:12 RSV).

In his second epistle, too, Peter affirmed the inspiration of scripture through the offices of the Holy Spirit:

Above all, you must understand that no prophecy of Scripture came about by the prophet's own interpretation. For prophecy never had its origin in the will of man, but men spoke from God as they were carried along by the Holy Spirit (2 Peter 1:20,21 NIV).

V. THE SPIRIT WORKED DIRECTLY IN THE EARLY CHURCH. While Barnabas and Saul were worshiping and praying with the church at Antioch, the Holy Spirit said, "Set apart for me Barnabas and Saul for the work to which I have called them." In obedience, the church fasted and prayed, and the leaders laid their hands on them and sent them off (Acts 13:2,3 NIV). In the following verse we find that the two were "sent on their way by the Holy Spirit."

In his farewell speech to the elders of the church at Ephesus, Paul charged them to guard themselves and "all the flock of which the Holy Spirit has made you overseers" (Acts 20:28).

Not only did the Spirit send the preachers of the good news out, but he directed their travel. After Paul and Barnabas had separated, Paul took Silas with him. After visiting and strengthening the churches in Syria and Cilicia, they came to Derbe and Lystra. There they found young Timothy, whom they took with them on their mission. The Holy Spirit forbade their going into Asia; so they went to the regions of Phrygia and Galatia. From Mysia they tried to go into Bithynia, but the Spirit did not permit them to go. Instead, they were directed to go to Macedonia, where in Philippi Lydia and the jailer's household were converted. (Acts 16) In reading the Philippian letter we see what a blessing the Christians at Philippi were to Paul.

VI. THE MIRACULOUS GIFT OF THE SPIRIT WAS LIMITED. The ability to speak in other languages and to perform miracles was imparted for the purpose of confirming the word. It was transmitted by the laying on of the apostles' hands. When Peter and John were sent by the other apostles to Samaria, they laid their hands on the baptized believers that they might receive the Holy Spirit. Simon the sorcerer had gained much attention from the populace as he practiced his magic arts, but he had not seen anything like the power transmitted by the apostles. He heard their preaching and was baptized, but he got into trouble. Seeing that the Spirit was bestowed by the laying on of the apostles' hands, he tried to buy their power so that he could also convey the Spirit to those on whom he laid his hands. Peter informed him in no uncertain terms that this power could not be bought and told him to repent and pray to be forgiven. Immediately he asked that they pray with him (Acts 8:9-24).

Since this special measure of the Spirit, given for the purpose of confirming the word as it was being recorded, was transmitted by the laying on of the apostles' hands, it is reasonable to conclude that it ceased when those on whom it had been bestowed finished their work. We now have the recorded word that we might believe (John 20:30,31).

VII. THE SCRIPTURES TEACH THAT THE SPIRIT IS ALIVE AND ACTIVE. It is a rather common mistake to assume, since the Spirit had a special work to do as the apostles were being inspired to remember and to carry out the will of Jesus Christ, that he is not active in the lives of each baptized believer who has been added to the body of Christ. In ignoring the Spirit we are depriving ourselves of the help intended by the Father and Son.

A. Isaiah cried out, "Where is He who put his Holy Spirit in the midst of them?" (Isaiah 63:11 NASV).

Isaiah recounted the goodness of God as he brought them out of Egyptian bondage, how He was afflicted with them, redeemed them in love and mercy. Yet he laments, "But they rebelled and grieved His Holy Spirit; therefore, He turned Himself to become their enemy, He fought against them" (Isaiah 63:10).

Can we assume that the Holy Spirit is not grieved today when we rebel?

B. In his masterful recounting of the history of Israel, Stephen brought a resounding accusation against the Jews who were resisting the spread of the gospel:

You stiff-necked people, with uncircumcised hearts and ears! You are just like your fathers: You always resist the Holy Spirit! Was there ever a prophet your fathers did not persecute? They even killed those who predicted the coming of the Righteous One. And now you have betrayed and murdered him--you who have received the law that was put into effect through angels but have not obeyed it (Acts 7:51-53 NIV).

Are we any less guilty of resisting the Spirit if we fail to know and obey God's will as revealed through Christ and the Holy Spirit?

C. In Ephesians chapter four, Paul urges Christians to live a life worthy of their calling, to get rid of un-Christlike attitudes and actions. He appeals to them and us, "You were taught with regard to your former way of life, to put off your old self, which is being corrupted by its deceitful desires; to be made new in the attitude of your minds; and to put on the new self, created to be like God in true righteousness and holiness" (Ephesians 4:22,23 NIV).

As a clinching admonition for the new way of life, Paul urged, "And do not grieve the Holy Spirit of God, with whom you were sealed for the day of redemption" (Ephesians 4:30 NIV).

After becoming Christians, do we grieve the Holy Spirit when we hold onto the old way of life, fail to live a life worthy of Christ?

D. In writing to the church at Thessalonica, Paul even indicates that Christians, by their lives, may "put out the Spirit's fire." He urged them to be alert and self-controlled, to be joyful, pray continually, give thanks always. He concluded, "Do not quench the Spirit, do not despise prophesying, but test everything; hold fast what is good, abstain from every form of evil" (1 Thessalonians 5:19,20 RSV).

If it had not been possible for Christians to live lives which would put out the Spirit's flame--nullify His influence in our lives--would Paul have recorded this stern warning to be read by Christians in all times and places?

VIII. HOW DOES THE HOLY SPIRIT AFFECT THE LIVES OF CHRISTIANS? First, let us make amply clear that in no way does the Spirit contradict the word of God. Jesus said, "Not everyone that saith unto me, Lord, Lord, shall enter into the kingdom of heaven; but he that doeth the will of my Father which is in heaven (Matthew 7:21 KJ). Faith comes by hearing the word of

God (Romans 10:17). Remember that the household of Cornelius was commanded to be baptized in the name of Jesus Christ after having received the baptism of the Holy Spirit; this was to convince the Jews that the Gentiles were to be received into the kingdom; their obedience in baptism put them into the kingdom. Through the recorded word the Spirit guides us to obedience. We do have indications of his power and help in our lives. It is not for us to ask, "How, Lord?" That is God's business; we are to obey and accept.

A. In his sermon on the day of Pentecost, Peter revealed the promise of the gift of the Holy Spirit to baptized believers, and the promise was to those listening, to their children, and "to all that are afar off" (Acts 2:38,39). That would include us.

B. He dwells in Christians. There has been much discussion of "bodily indwelling." Again, we are safe to leave the *how* to God. Our concern should be to be a temple suitable for his dwelling. Paul said, "Do you not know that your body is a temple of the Holy Spirit, who is in you, whom you have received from God?" (1 Corinthians 6:19 NIV).

C. In the eighth chapter of Romans, Paul emphasizes the obligation of Christians, in whom the Spirit dwells, to "walk not after the flesh, but after the Spirit." He says, "For if you live according to the sinful nature, you will die; but if by the Spirit you put to death the misdeeds of the body, you will live, because those who are led by the Spirit of God are sons of God" (Romans 8:13,14 NIV).

In this same chapter Paul presents the Spirit as one who helps those trying to overcome the fleshly nature:

> Likewise the Spirit helps us in our weakness; for we do not know how to pray as we ought, but the Spirit himself intercedes for us with sighs too deep for words. And he who searches the hearts of men knows what is the mind of the Spirit, because the Spirit intercedes for the saints according to the will of God (Romans 8:26,27 RSV).

D. Those who are spiritually minded bear the fruit of the Spirit. Never is it indicated that the Spirit relieves Christians of their duty to overcome the temptations of the flesh. Paul urged the Galatians to "walk by the Spirit, and do not gratify the desires of the flesh...those who belong to Christ Jesus have crucified the flesh with its passions and desires" (Galatians 5:16, 24 RSV). Between these two verses Paul has listed the works of the flesh, which are to be avoided because "those who do such things shall not inherit the kingdom of God."

Listed as fruit of the Spirit are: love, joy, peace, patience, kindness, goodness, faithfulness, gentleness, and self-control. Not only are these goals for the Spirit-filled life, but they are the result of such a life (Galatians 5:16-25).

E. Paul shows that both Jew and Gentile are joint heirs in Christ and in the same way are recipients of the Holy Spirit as a seal, a guarantee. Although he expressed almost the same in other scriptures, he left no doubt of the Spirit's "seal" when he wrote:

In him we were also chosen, having been predestined according to the plan of him who works out everything in conformity with the purpose of his will, in order that we, who were the first to hope in Christ, might be fore the praise of his glory. And you also were included in Christ when you heard the word of truth, the gospel of your salvation. Having believed, you were marked in him with a seal, the promised Holy Spirit, who is a deposit guaranteeing our inheritance until the redemption of those who are God's possession--to the praise of his glory. (Ephesians 1:11-14, NIV; See also Romans 8:14-16; 2 Corinthians 1:21,22; Galatians 4:6; 1 John 4:13)

CONCLUSION: Actually, we may only have "touched the hem of the garment" in our efforts really to know God, Christ, and the Holy Spirit. But we do know that only through prayerful and diligent study of the inspired word can we begin to comprehend the marvelous things they have in store for us. While the foolish woman ignores God's word and walks after the flesh, the wise woman trusts and obeys and is confident of that sealed to her by the Holy Spirit.

Paul's plea for the Corinthians is mine for each of you: "May the grace of the Lord Jesus Christ, and the love of God, and the fellowship of the Holy Spirit be with you all" (2 Corinthians 13:14 NIV).

DAILY BIBLE READINGS:
Sunday: Acts 7, Stephen's picture of those who resist the Spirit
Monday: John 14, Jesus promises the Holy Spirit.
Tuesday: Ephesians 4, Living as children of light
Wednesday: Romans 8, Life through the Spirit
Thursday: Acts 13, Guided by the Spirit
Friday: John 16:5-15, The work of the Holy Spirit
Saturday: 2 Corinthians 1:18-22; Galatians 3:26 to 4:6; 1 John 3:21-24, 4:13, Sealed by the Holy Spirit
MEMORY VERSES: 2 Peter 1:20,21

Chapter 5

The Wise Woman Knows
HERSELF

We hear much talk today about "self-realization." Seminars are held by "experts" in an effort to help those attending "discover self," free one's self from guilt perhaps by changing the rules. The total emphasis is the exaltation of *self*; it amounts almost to Narcissism, worship of self.

It is true that we must, in a sense, know who we are and where we're going. Otherwise we can drift aimlessly through life, accomplishing very little and failing to find satisfaction and true happiness.

When we want to know how to operate a new microwave oven, we go to the manual put out by its maker. If you really want to know your most glorious self, go to the book inspired by your Maker. It may sound like a paradox, but you will find that the fulfilled life is one that *has lost self*.

I. TAKE A LOOK AT SELF. Just who are you? Psychologists tell us that a person is the product of combined heredity and environment.

The color of your hair and eyes, your physical build are determined by a complex system of genes inherited from your parents. There is very little we can do about some of these; others may be changed cosmetically, even to the extent of plastic surgery. Perhaps some of your emotional tendencies may be inherited.

It is hard, however, to determine just which of our attitudes are inherent and which have been acquired through our environment. We may have a poor self-image because we have been belittled by parents, siblings, or peers. We may be egotistical because we have been showered with constant attention and praise, perhaps beyond what we deserve.

You must not be a slave either to heredity or environment. You are not locked into a pattern of thought or action over which you can have no control. Do not become so concerned with the attainment of physical goals that you forget to set spiritual goals. Some times there will be conflicts between the two. The Apostle Paul describes this struggle dramatically in Romans 7 and points the way to escape.

> I find then a law, that, when I would do good, evil is present with me. For I delight in the law of God after the inward man: But I see another law in my members, warring against the law of my mind, and bringing me into captivity to the law of sin which is in my members. O wretched man that I am! who shall deliver me from the body of this death? I thank God through Jesus Christ our Lord. So then with the mind I myself serve the law of God; but with the flesh the law of sin. There is therefore now no condemnation to them which are in Christ Jesus, who walk not after the flesh, but after the Spirit. For the law of the Spirit of life in Christ Jesus hath made me free from the law of sin and death (Romans 7:21-8:2 KJ).

This new life in Christ is readily available to you--without regard to your heredity, environment, or social situation. Your New Testament tells you plainly how you may become a "new you" in Christ.

II. HOW IS THIS NEW SELF ACHIEVED? First, you must realize a need for change. While you may have been living a good life in the eyes of the world, you must realize that in Christ you will be right in the sight of God. With a pure and honest heart, seek truth from God's word then be willing to follow your Maker's prescription.

A. Do not deceive yourself. In describing the sinfulness of the wicked, the Psalmist said, "There is no fear of God before his eyes, For in his own eyes he flatters himself too much to detect or hate his sin" (Psalms 36:2 NIV). In other words, you can not see beyond self. Or it might be more accurate to say you may not be objective enough to see your real self.

1. No one is capable of reconciliation to God through her own righteousness. It is reasonable to suppose that God chose the household of Cornelius as the first Gentiles to hear the gospel because of his righteousness. We are told, "He and all his family were devout and God-fearing; he gave generously to those in need and prayed to God regularly" (Acts 10:2 NIV). Yet by a miracle God convinced Peter, a Jew, that he should go and preach to this good family. They certainly were not what we consider vile sinners, yet they were not in Christ. They needed the cleansing of his blood, to be made new in Christ.

2. "All have sinned and come short of the glory of God," Paul said in Romans 3:23. He had said in previous verses that both Jews and Gentiles are alike under sin. We are in need of redemption.

Here, again, there is danger of self-deception. "If we claim to be without sin, we deceive ourselves and the truth is not in us. If we confess our sins, he is faithful and just and will forgive us our sins and purify us from all unrighteousness. If we claim we have not sinned, we make him out to be a liar and his word has no place in our lives" (1 John 1:8-10 NIV).

B. RECEIVE. POWER TO BECOME A CHILD OF GOD. You have not seen George Washington or Abraham Lincoln, but you believe they lived and helped to establish and maintain the government under which we now live. You believe because you had read accounts of their lives by those who have examined the evidence pertaining to them. In the same way you may come to know Jesus Christ. Matthew, Mark, Luke, and John did not have to dig through musty files for their evidence; each had been associated closely with Jesus and could say, as John said of himself, "This is the disciple who testifies to these things and who wrote them down. We know that his testimony is true" (John 21:24 NIV).

John describes Jesus as the Word, who was with God in the beginning yet was made flesh and lived among men for a while. He tells how Jesus, himself, declared he is the Way, the Truth, and the Life; that no one comes unto the Father but by himself. "He came to his own home, and his own people received him not. But to all who received him, who believed in his name, he gave power to become children of God," John wrote in the first chapter of his story of Jesus, verse 12.

Having heard and believed the evidence, you have the right, or power, to become a child of God!

C. DO AN ABOUT-FACE. Once, on a cloudy day, my husband and I were trying to go from New York City to Boston. We got on what we believed to be the right, divided toll road and were congratulating ourselves that we were not going the opposite direction, where traffic was so heavy. We ignored a souvenir compass which indicated we were going in the wrong direction, deciding the cheap thing was just not accurate.

Arriving at a toll gate, we asked, "Is this the road to Boston?"

"Yes," the attendant replied, "BUT you are going in the wrong direction."

We then were convinced we were wrong, on the basis of this authoritative evidence. We believed, but we still had to make the move necessary: exit, pay a toll, and turn around in order to go in the right direction. Continuing in this way, we arrived safely at our destination.

Though you may have lived a GOOD life, you still may need to change the direction of your life, to dedicate it to the Lord; that is conversion. How refreshing it can be, when we have been convinced we have been wrong, to be able to turn and make a fresh start. Peter put it this way, "Repent, therefore, and turn again, that your sins may be blotted out, that times of refreshing may come from the presence of the Lord" (Acts 3:19 RSV).

D. OWN CHRIST AS LORD. For those of us who have been reared by believing parents it is not hard to confess that Jesus Christ is the Son of God. However, our faith must be our own; we must have been convinced by the Word that he is Lord. We must be willing to let him direct our lives. With our mouths and in our lives we must confess him: "Whoever, therefore, shall confess me before men, him will I confess also before my Father which is in heaven. But whosoever shall deny me before men, him will I also deny before my Father which is in heaven" (Matthew 10:32 KJ).

Wouldn't you be thrilled if your senator were so well pleased with something you had done that he commended you to the president of the United States? How much greater honor it is to have Jesus Christ confess *our name* before the God of the Universe!

E. DIE TO SIN: RISE TO LIFE ON A NEW PLANE. What could be more meaningful to one who, because of her belief in Jesus as Christ, her repentance of sin, and her confession of her Lord, is determined to live a new life than a reenactment of the death, burial, and resurrection of Jesus? That is exactly what baptism is. It would be gruesome to bury one who is alive; it is futile to go through the form of baptism without being willing to turn from sin, give up self, belong to Christ.

Paul wrote, "We died to sin; how can we live in it any longer? Or don't you know that all of us who were baptized into Christ Jesus were baptized into his death? We were therefore buried with him through baptism into death in order that, just as Christ was raised from the dead through the glory of the Father, we too may live a new life" (Romans 6:2-4 NIV).

This passage makes it very plain that baptism is not merely an ordinance of the church to show we have been saved. It is, actually, the death of the person of sin and the birth into Christ – into a fresh, new life. Just before his ascension, Jesus commanded that those who were taught must be baptized; then more teaching must be done: "All authority in heaven and on earth has been given to me. Go therefore and make disciples of all nations, baptizing them in the name of the Father and of the Son and of the Holy Spirit, teaching them to observe all that I have commanded you" (Matthew 28:18-20a RSV).

III. MEET THE NEW YOU! This new creation may resemble the old you in many ways, but you must never forget that you are no longer living for self but for Christ, who loved us enough to die for us. We love him enough to live for him. Paul explained it this way:

> For the love of Christ controls us, because we are convinced that one has died for all; therefore all have died. And he died for all, that those who live might live no longer for themselves but for him who for their sake died and was raised. From now on, therefore, we regard no one from a human point of view; even though we once regarded Christ from a human point of view, we regard him thus no longer. Therefore, if any one is in Christ, he is a new creation; the old has passed away, behold, the new has come. (2 Corinthians 5:14-17 RSV)

A. As a "babe in Christ" you must crucify the flesh, walk by the Spirit. Do not be discouraged if there is conflict between the two. Remember that, with the Lord's help, you will have power to overcome the temptations Satan will throw at you to try to win you back to his ways.

1. Keep yourself free from guilt. When you were born anew, you were cleansed from all your past sins. The Lord has forgiven you; you must forgive yourself. This does not mean that you may not have to bear the consequences of some sin, but it does mean that you are free from the guilt of sin. Quite often a person serving a long sentence in the pentitentiary is taught then baptized into Christ. She is a new creation and can live in the Spirit and in the prison walls at the same time. While she may not have physical freedom, she has spiritual freedom. This is freedom indeed! Jesus said, "If the Son makes you free, you will be free indeed" (John 8:36 RSV).

But what if you sin after becoming a Christian? Your Bible answers that question, too. Remember that Simon, the sorcerer, believed and was baptized. Then he sinned by trying to buy the gift of the Spirit so that he could impart spiritual gifts as the apostles did by the laying on of hands. Peter told him to repent of his wickedness and pray for forgiveness, (Acts 8:14-24).

Your cleansing from sin can be a continual process. Jesus said that he is the light of the world. John wrote, "If we walk in the light, as He Himself is in the light, we have fellowship with one another, and the blood of Jesus His Son cleanses us from all sin" (1 John 1:7 NASV). Fellowship with Christ and with other Christians through regular worship and communion, study and prayer, will help you walk in the light. When you contacted the blood of Christ in baptism, you were cleansed from past sins; his blood *cleanses* you from sin. Note the *present, active* tense of the verb. As you are walking in the light, you are being cleansed from all sin.

2. Your life will have new meaning as you grow in Christ, walk in the Spirit. Your viewpoint is changed. Where you once loved things of the world, you now love the Lord, things spiritual. Paul admonishes:

> Since then you have been raised with Christ, set your hearts on things above, where Christ is seated at the right hand of God. Set your minds on things above, not on earthly things. For you have died, and your life is hidden with Christ in God. When Christ, who is your life, appears, then you also will appear with him in glory (Colossians 3:1-4 NIV).

"Having purified your souls by your obedience to the truth," Peter writes, "put away all malice and all guile and insincerity and envy and slander. Like newborn babes, long for the pure spiritual milk, that by it you may grow up to salvation" (1 Peter 1:22a;2:1,2 RSV; Note that the King James translation says, "desire the sincere milk of the word").

3. As Paul indicated in Romans 7, the struggle between the carnal and spiritual is a continuing battle, even after one has surrendered her life to Christ. Remember, Jesus said, "If any man will come after me, let him deny himself, and take up his cross, and follow me. For whosoever will save his life shall lose it: and whosoever will lose his life for my sake shall find it. For what is a man profited, if he shall gain the whole world, and lose his own soul? or what shall a man give in exchange for his soul?" (Matthew 16:24-26 KJ).

This denial of the old self is described well as we continue in Paul's letter to the Colossians:

> Put to death, therefore, whatever belongs to your earthly nature: sexual immorality, impurity, lust, evil desires and

greed, which is idolatry. Because of these, the wrath of God is coming. You used to walk in these ways, in the life you once lived. But now you must rid yourselves of all such things as these: anger, rage, malice, slander, and filthy language from your lips. Do not lie to each other, since you have taken off your old self with its practices and have put on the new self, which is being renewed in knowledge in the image of its Creator...Therefore as God's chosen people, holy and dearly loved, clothe yourselves with compassion, kindness, humility, gentleness and patience. Bear with each other and forgive whatever grievances you may have against one another. Forgive as the Lord forgave you. And over all these virtues put on love, which binds them all together in perfect unity. (Colossians 3:5-10;12-14 NIV)

You have taken off your old self, with its carnal ways, and have put on a brand new self. Note how this self is given daily renewal: in knowledge, gained by daily study of God's word; and in the image of its Creator, by following Christ's example as we learn more of him in our study and meditation. The list of Christian attributes given above is very similar to the fruit of the Spirit as listed by Paul in Galatians 5:22,23.

Love is an essential in the Christ-like life. One of the great commandments, as quoted by Christ, was "Love your neighbor as yourself." But Jesus also gave a new commandment: "Love each other as I have loved you. Greater love has no one than this, that one lay down his life for his friends. You are my friends if you do what I command you" (John 15:12-14 NIV).

B. YOU'RE NOW A CHILD OF THE KING--A PRINCESS! Your old self may have projected a poor self-image. Your new image is glorious. Off with self doubt and insecurity! The life in Christ is full of assurance, confidence. You are in a new family relationship, full of love, joy, and peace.

1. None but the high priest could enter the Holy Place in the old Jewish tabernacle. As a Christian, you are now a priest in that you can go directly to God through Christ, our high priest. You were added to the Lord's body, the church, when you were raised from baptism to walk the new life with him. The writer of Hebrews refers to Christians as a "holy priesthood," and reveals that they are free to enter the fellowship of saints:

Therefore, brothers, since we have confidence to enter the Most Holy Place by the blood of Jesus, by a new and living way opened for us through the curtain, that is, his body, and since we have a great priest over the house of God, let us draw near to God with a sincere heart in full assurance of faith, having our hearts sprinkled to cleanse us from a guilty conscience and having our bodies washed with pure water.Let us hold unswervingly to the hope we profess, for he who promised is faithful. And let us consider how we may spur one another on toward love and good deeds. Let us not give up meeting together, as some are in the habit of doing, but let us encourage one another--and all the more as you see the Day approaching (Hebrews 10:19-25 NIV).

Confidence and assurance, then, come to you in Christ. He planned that we meet together regularly to remember the sacrifice he made for us and to encourage each other. This is necessary to your spiritual growth; if you forsake the assembly, you certainly will lose confidence, become weak, perhaps fall away all together.

2. You are now in a loving, new family relationship--your forever family! God is your Father; you are a joint heir with Christ. Your Father owns the world! He loves you so much that he gave his Son that you might have eternal life (John 3:16). The magnitude of God's love is almost beyond our comprehension. John's later letters are full of teaching about that love: "How great is the love the Father has lavished on us, that we should be called children of God! And that is what we are! The reason the world does not know us is that it did not know him. Dear friends, now we are children of God" (1 John 3:1,2 NIV).

You can go to your heavenly Father in prayer just as you made requests of your earthly father. He cares about you and wants you to talk to him about your everyday needs, although he knows and plans to supply your daily necessities. Better than an earthly father, He knows how to give good gifts to his children. He also, like a conscientious earthly father, will continue to care for us, requiring only that we love and obey him (Matthew 6:25-34;7:9-11).

Your earthly family is actually a cohesive unit for a relatively short time. Brothers and sisters grow up, go off to college, go off to establish their own homes often in far-away places. Parents at best can protect us for only a short time; then you leave them or they are taken away by death. But the Lord's family is everlasting! It is God's will that you be able to find brothers and sisters in Christ wherever you may live or travel. One of the greatest joys my husband and I have known has been in worshiping with our brothers and sisters in small, far-away places who were hungering for the Christian fellowship we so often take for granted.If your occupation or your husband's should take you where you find no Christian family, you possess the means--God's word--to make them your brothers and sisters, to share with them the joy you have found in your new self. If you yet lack the confidence to teach them, you have loving brothers and sisters in the Lord who can and will help you.

Remember, Jesus said, "Here are my mother and my brothers!" He was indicating his disciples. Then he added, "For whoever does the will of my Father in heaven is my brother, and sister, and mother" (Matthew 12:49,50).

CONCLUSION: The foolish woman trudges along with her old self, full of uncertainty and self-doubt. The wise woman crucifies her old self and finds the new life in Christ gives her a new identity, gloriously fulfilled.

DAILY BIBLE READINGS:
Sunday: Acts 9:1-22, An about face.
Monday: 1 Timothy 1:12-17, Eternal life to the chief of sinners.
Tuesday: Galatians 2:15-20, Alive in Christ.
Wednesday: Romans 8:1-17, Now no condemnation.
Thursday: Romans 8:18-38, More than conquerors.
Friday: Matthew 12:46-50, Your "forever family."
Saturday: Mark 10:28-30, Showers of blessings.
MEMORY VERSE: Galatians 2:20

Chapter 6

The Wise Woman Knows
HER ROLE

"The part one plays in life" is a simple but adequate definition of *role*. Because of the continuing confusion of male and female roles in our present day society, it seems necessary that those of us who want to please God know and respect woman's role as it is presented in the scriptures. Although this role has been discussed in previous writing, I make no apology for its perusal here; we dare neglect no opportunity to help each other to know the Lord's will, obey it, and live triumphant, happy lives.

Children understand what is meant when they are assigned roles in a school play. Each knows that she is to learn her part and play it to the best of her ability as a member of the cast. The play will be a disaster if Mary spends all her time concentrating on Joe's role, wanting to play his part. She also can damage the effectiveness of the play if she tries to play the minor role as if she were the prima dona. Or, in stage lingo, if she "up-stages" others during their scenes. The minor roles are important; the play would be incomplete without them; but they must be played in relation to the whole. It is the director who assigns the roles and helps each actor to play her part in a convincing manner so that the play will be a success.

In the roles we play as Christians, God is the director. In fact, by inspiring godly men, he wrote the script. Our part is to accept our own role and play it as he directs. Even the smallest Christian role is greater than that of the prophets. Jesus said, "Truly, I say to you, among those born of women there has risen no one greater than John the Baptist; yet he who is least in the kingdom of heaven is greater than he" (Matthew 11:11 RSV). What a challenge to give it our best!

The charge made by some feminists that God made woman as an afterthought, a poor copy of man and inferior to him is completely without substance. We can not deny, however, that both man and woman were given distinctive roles and that each is happier when those differences are respected. That woman was created to be a "helper suited to him" does not make woman inferior to man. As Reuel Lemmons has said so aptly in the *Firm Foundation* of Sept. 26, 1978:

> Nowhere in the Bible is a woman enjoined or commanded to take authority over a man. This does not make woman a second class citizen. It simply relegates her to the position on the team where God decrees that she should play her part. She is, and can never be otherwise, a second class man; just as man could never be anything better than a second class woman. Women are created to be women and men are created to be men. Nothing can change that. Neither ought to want it changed. Woman's primary ministry differs from that of man, and she should be glad that in her realm she is supreme.

That she was made a helper does not indicate that God intended that woman should be a slave or that she should be mistreated by man. God's loving arrangement provides care for woman from girlhood to womanhood, as wives or widows. He demands respect for womanhood. Fathers are given the responsibility of bringing up their children "in the nurture and admonition of the Lord" (Ephesians 6:4). "Husbands, love your wives as Christ loved the church and gave himself for it," Paul wrote the Ephesians (Ephesians 5:25). And in 1 Timothy 5 the same inspired writer gives detailed instruction for the care of widows.

I. In this day of role confusion, Christian women need to know their role and teach their daughters how to be women pleasing to God. The scriptures are plain in outlining God's plan for us.

A. That woman was not an afterthought is shown by God's statement of purpose: "It is not good that the man should be alone; I will make him a helper fit for him" (Genesis 2:18 RSV). Apparently, man and woman were given joint dominion over the living creatures.

> So God created man in his own image, in the image of God he created him; male and female he created them. And God blessed them, and God said to them, "Be fruitful and multiply, and fill the earth and subdue it; and have dominion over the fish of the sea and over the birds of the air and over every living thing that moves upon the earth" (Genesis 1:27,28 RSV).

B. Woman's supportive role came about as a result of her own actions. She was placed with her husband in the beautiful Garden of

Eden. She knew that they were free to eat of its bounty with one exception; they were not to eat from the tree of the knowledge of good and evil...the tree in the middle of the garden, as Eve described it to Satan. Then she listened to the serpent; she rationalized.

"When the woman saw that the tree was good for food, and that it was a delight to the eyes, and that the tree was desirable to make one wise, she took from its fruit and ate; and she gave also to her husband with her, and he ate" (Genesis 3:6 NASV).

God, because of her action and Satan's deception, pronounced a curse on the serpent and told the man and woman of their changed relationship to him and to each other.

There would be enmity between the serpent and the woman; between his seed and her seed, "He shall bruise you on the head, And you shall bruise him on the the heel." We understand that this is the prophecy of the coming of the Christ, who would restore mankind to convenant relationship with God.

Man would no longer be able to live innocently in the beautiful garden but would have to fight weeds, thorns and thistles for his living. Woman would bring forth her children in multiplied pain, yet she would desire her husband, and he would rule over her.

C. That woman is to be in subjection to man is taught in the New Testament, where it is pointed out that this is true because she was deceived. Paul wrote to Timothy:

> Let a woman learn in silence with all submissiveness. I permit no woman to teach or to have authority over men; she is to keep silent. For Adam was formed first, then Eve; and Adam was not deceived, but the woman was deceived and became a transgressor (1 Timothy 2:11-14 RSV).

We as women should not, however, think that we are the only ones who must learn submission. Christians in general are told to be subject one to another. Man certainly must be subject to Christ, and even Christ learned obedience as a son. Paul listed the order: "But I would have you know, that the head of every man is Christ; and the head of the woman is the man; and the head of Christ is God" (1 Corinthians 11:3 KJ).

In this passage the Revised Standard Version says, "The head of a woman is her husband." Both Paul and Peter taught that wives are to be submissive to their husbands, and each emphasized that the husband is to love his wife, to be considerate of her.

Paul wrote the Colossians: "Wives, submit yourselves unto your own husbands, as it is fit in the Lord." To the husbands he says, "Husbands, love your wives, and be not bitter against them" (Colossians 3:18,19 KJ). He repeats the same admonition to the Ephesians, comparing the husband-wife relationship to that of Christ and the church.

After making a strong appeal to Christians to follow Christ's example of submission, Peter wrote:

> Likewise you wives, be submissive to your husbands, so that some, though they do not obey the word, may be won without a word by the behavior of their wives, when they see your reverent and chaste behavior...Likewise you husbands, live considerately with your wives, bestowing honor on the woman as the weaker sex, since you are joint heirs of the grace of life, in order that your prayers may not be hindered. (1 Peter 3:1,2,7 RSV)

Actually, it might be more practical to say we are considering the roles women play, plural, not singular. We will go into that later. First, though, we want to establish that "women are women; men are men." We must emphasize that we are not saying that woman has a lesser role than man; simply that God has assigned her a different role both in woman-man and God-man-woman relationships. Although some deprecate this fact and insist on equality, per se, it is my conviction that experience shows and Bible study confirms that we are happiest, most useful to the Master when we respect our feminine sexuality and explore all facets of our life in God's framework. May I quote again from the article by Reuel Lemmons:

> To both creations God gave special and specific assignments. These assignments cannot be ignored without penalty. It has been so since the beginning. It will ever be so...God has endowed man with a sphere of authority and all the amendments in the world will never change that. God has given woman a sphere of influence and of authority and all the laws we humans pass will not dethrone God, nor set aside his mandate.

II. Just what, then, is woman's "sphere of influence and authority?" Here we may go into the changing roles a woman plays as she progresses from childhood to old age.

A. "It's a girl!" is the answer to perhaps the most asked question when a baby is born: "Is it a boy or a girl?" We know that the tone, the amount of excitement evident in the answer may depend on the newborn's older siblings. If they are boys, faces light up when the doctor says, "It's a girl." However, if she is the third, fourth, sixth or seventh female child, even family members may look dejected when they make the pronouncement. How fortunate, though, that each has her own personality, that sisters and parents usually exclaim later, "Whatever would we have done without her?"

B. Her continuing role, as long as she or her parents live, is that of daughter. Some may insist that society forces her into the stereotyped feminine role. Really, can we believe that, assuming good health and a normal amount of acceptance, that tradition has anything to do with the way she develops a special ability to use her softness and sweetness to "wrap daddy around her little finger?" What God expects of her as a child, though, is to learn to obey and respect her parents.

"Children, obey your parents in the Lord, for this is right. 'Honor your father and mother'--which is the first commandment with promise--'that it may go well with you and that you may enjoy long life on the earth.' " is the instruction given through Paul (Ephesians 6:1,2 NIV).

Who is most likely to care for ill or aging parents? Usually it is a daughter, even if there are many sons in the family. When a girl marries, she takes on a new role as daughter-in-law. This new relationship can be warm and loving or jealous and defiant, depending on the maturity and Christianity of both women involved. At times it is a daughter-in-law who comforts an aging parent. We think of Ruth and Naomi as the ideal mother-daughter-in-law relationship. If we notice carefully, we see that each showed kindness and consideration to the other. We don't find Naomi referring to them as "my sons' wives."

When they insisted on going with her from Moab to Judah, after the death of her husband and sons, she counseled: "Go, return each of you to her mother's house. May the Lord deal kindly with you, as you have dealt with the dead and with me."

At their persistence, she spoke to them as if they had been her own flesh and blood: "Turn back, my daughters, why will you go with me?"

Others saw Ruth's devotion to Naomi. They said at the birth of an heir: "He shall be to you a restorer of life and a nourisher of your old age; for your daughter-in-law who loves you, who is more to you than seven sons, has borne him" (Ruth 1:8,11; 4:15 RSV).

C. Perhaps in all cultures young women are expected to marry, to become wives. Until recent times, she may not have had a choice in the tradition under which she was born. Although the scriptures do confirm that woman was first created as a helper suited to man, and Eve became the wife of Adam, there is some evidence later that a woman was given a choice. When Abraham sent his servant back to his country, to his kindred, to find a wife for Isaac, he prayed for guidance from the Lord. Rebekah seemed to him and her parents to be the one chosen by the Lord. However, when the servant wished to depart the following morning, her brother and mother said, "We will call the maiden and ask her." "They called Rebekah and asked her, 'Will you go with this man?' She said, 'I will go' " (Genesis 24:57, 58).

We have no evidence that Miriam, the sister of Moses and Aaron, was married. We first see her, perhaps as a little girl, when she watched by the river and brought her mother to care for baby Moses at the request of the princess. She worked closely with them during the wilderness wanderings and was referred to as "Miriam the prophetess" (Exodus 15:20). Among the women who followed Jesus and ministered to him were women of substance. Although one or more may have been married, we actually are not told of their marital status. Suffice it to say that among the most dedicated Christians today are many women who serve alone. Some by choice or circumstance never have married. Others are widows. During the past decade or two we find in America less pressure being put on young women to marry. Many are choosing to live singly, and they should not be condemned so long as they are faithful to the Lord.

Paul recognized that not everyone could live the celibate life he chose, saying "Let every one lead the life which the Lord has assigned him, and in which God has called him. This is my rule in all the Churches" (1 Corinthians 7:17). He has given instruction on the mutual responsibilities of husbands and wives, and has indicated that a Christian can serve married or single. However, he counseled:

> I want you to be free from anxieties...the unmarried woman or girl is anxious about the affairs of the Lord, how to be holy in body and spirit; but the married woman is anxious about worldly affairs, how to please her husband. I say this for your own benefit, not to lay any restraint upon you, but to promote good order and to secure your undivided devotion to the Lord. (1 Corinthians 7:32,34-35 RSV)

D. A woman who chooses to marry assumes a new role that of WIFE. Unlike the woman who remains single, her life is bound up in that of another; she and he have become one. As Paul indicated above, one of her responsibilities is to please her husband. This includes every facet of her life, physical, emotional, and spiritual. In the chapter from which we read above, Paul says plainly that both husband and wife are obligated to fulfill the other's sexual needs. The only reason he gives for denial, and then it is by consent, is to devote oneself to prayer, and then they are to come together again to avoid temptation.

Not too much is said in the scriptures about woman's role as homemaker...and of course she can be a home maker, whether or not she is married. The married woman's role here is more demanding, since she is making a home for her husband and perhaps children. In Titus 2:5 we have the succinct statement that older women are to teach the younger to be keepers at home, domestic, home lovers, or busy at home, depending on the translation being studied. As in all areas, the Lord expects us to do well in all we undertake. Older women, from their experience, are to help the younger in this and other areas.

The home certainly is the woman's sphere of influence and authority. The setting of guidelines and budgets must be a joint effort of husband and wife, but the execution usually is her responsibility. We recognize that in some households today this order is being reversed, but by nature most women have the patience with detail necessary in doing the planning of menus, cooking of food, shopping, and cleaning essential to a satisfactory home life. If she does not actually do the work, hers is the responsibility to see that it is done, whether by children or hired help, or even with the assistance of the husband.

Again we turn to Paul's writing: "I will therefore that the younger women marry, bear children, guide the house, give none occasion to the adversary to speak reproachfully" (1 Timothy 5:14 KJ). The Revised Standard says "rule their households." Phillips says "run their own households," and in a more genteel manner the New English says "preside over a home." In any case, we get the point that this is her realm of authority, the place where she is queen.

E. If a home is blessed with children, a woman's new role is MOTHER. Let us hasten to note that several of her roles are played simultaneously. She can and must be daughter, wife, citizen, Christian, and mother at the same time. All must recognize that there are stages in her life when one role must be somewhat dominant, as is true of the mother with young children. Even if she chooses to work outside the home, she must see that her children receive loving, constant care. But she must not forget that she also has a Lord and a husband to please, although in caring for the children she is serving both.

Among the many mothers of whom we read in the Bible, Hanna whose story is told in 1 Samuel 1 and 2, is a beautiful example. She was prayerful and self-denying. She prayed for a son then gave him unselfishly to the service of her God. She did not forget to thank the Lord for giving her this long-desired son; so she was rewarded with sons and daughters. She was industrious, making clothing for Samuel, and showed her love by visiting him and perhaps encouraging him in his work.

Luke gives us a graphic picture of Mary, the mother of Jesus. She was humble, obedient, willing to risk her reputation to be a handmaid of God. She was aware of all that was said about her son, all that he did, stored these things up in her heart. She followed him but apparently was willing to give place to others who were important in his life. Although she could have taken offense when he addressed her as "woman" at the wedding in Cana of Galilee, she told the servants, "Do whatever he tells you." She followed him to the cross and was rewarded by being entrusted by her son to the loving care of the disciple who loved him, John.

F. Although it seems to young mothers that the days of changing diapers and wiping noses will last forever, four to six short years slip by, and our woman finds herself free to devote more time to activities outside the home. More than one has had to be counseled by an older woman not to "spread herself too thin." It is an old saying but worthy of repetition: the good, if we are not careful, can crowd out the best. However, Christian women can, with discretion, improve the quality of life in their community, even their nation, by becoming involved. The Bible has examples of several such women.

The worthy woman of Proverbs 31 saw first to her home duties; then she became a business woman, buying land, planting a vineyard, selling garments to the merchants. Because of her support, her husband was influential among his peers.

Women have been through the ages especially adept in the field of benevolence. The worthy woman of Proverbs 31 opened her hand to the poor, stretched forth her hand to the needy. She accomplished this while seeing that her family was well fed and clothed; we are told she looked well to the ways of her household. The name of Dorcas is immortal because of her deeds of charity. Widows stood by

Peter and wept, showing him garments she had made. We are told that she did these deeds of kindness continually. Many became believers when they heard of her being raised from the dead.

Deborah, a married woman, was one of the judges of Israel. We are told in Judges 4 that she was the wife of Lappidoth and that she was a prophetess, and that the sons of Israel came up to her for judgment. Despite the assurance that God would deliver his enemies into his hands, the commander of her army, Barak, refused to go into battle unless she accompanied him. She agreed to go but warned him that Sisera would be delivered into the hands of a woman. We are told nothing of her home life, just that she was a wife, but we assume that she exercised wisdom in her home as well as in her judicial capacity.

Lydia, known as the first person Paul converted in Europe, was a business woman, a seller of purple from Thyatira. We do not know whether or not she was married, just that she and all her household were baptized when Paul preached to them at the riverside near Philippi. She was a worshiper of God and was with a group of women gathered for prayer when Paul and Silas spoke to them. She, too, must have been a good homemaker, for she begged the ministers of the gospel to come into her house and stay, which they did (Acts 16:13-15).

Women can serve in almost any capacity without losing their femininity. They must, however, remember and respect the Lord's plan for them.

III. Women find fulfillment and ample opportunity in the CHURCH. There is so much that we CAN do that very little needs to be said about what we can't do in the Lord's kingdom. I, for one, am thankful that God saw fit to put men in the leadership role. Yet no one will deny that much credit for the success of any program goes to the women who follow.

In the instructions given Timothy, chapter 3, and Titus, chapter 1, we see there is no way a woman can meet the qualifications for elder or deacon, both of whom must be "the husband of one wife." All the apostles were men, yet we read that they received much help from the women. The only restriction on women's service is that they not usurp authority over men. Again, Lemmons states it plainly:

> There are none of the works of the kingdom closed to women. The only restraint placed upon them is that they must not ururp the authority of man while engaged in these works. God authored this restriction. Man did not legislate it. Man cannot

annul it. A woman can sing. She can pray. She can teach. She can do anything a man can do in the kingdom. She simply must not usurp his authority, and get out of her place while doing it...Perhaps it should be said here, that man cannot abdicate. Some feel that if man gives permission, then woman can do anything. But the right to commission women to do what God has not commissioned them to do does not lie with men.

At one place where I taught a class for women during an area wide workshop, the printed program said simply that members of the faculty would make up the panel for a discussion in the assembly closing the day's activities. My husband and I, who was then still serving as an elder, discussed the situation. Since the elders had asked me to participate, would I be usurping authority? We decided that the safe course was to let the men handle the discussion. I felt much more comfortable as a member of the audience. I knew I was not setting a bad example for the women whom I had just taught.

Are you a teacher? Do you have executive ability? Every church has need for teachers in classes of children, girls, and women. You can work under the education director or an elder as supervisor of the various children's departments. No assignment is more challenging than eaching classes of teen-age girls, who are crying out for someone who has been there to help them solve some of the problems hurled at them by our permissive society. Nowhere are they more open and responsive than at the summer camp sessions when they are away from their usual environment. Some of the most effective classes are made up of women of all ages. You may teach your next door neighbor, the girl across the street. Through correspondence courses you may teach someone across town or across the ocean.

Can you sing? Children love to sing. Help them. You can enjoy the fellowship of Christians and serve the Lord while practicing with others so gifted to be ready to sing for weddings or funerals.

"I was sick and in prison, and you visited me," Jesus said to those on the right side in the judgment scene of Matthew 25. Your husband needs you to go with him to visit those in hospitals or who are ill at home. We must visit new comers and those who honor us with their presence at our serivces. Visiting need not be so organized that someone must tell us when and whom to visit. Our love prompts us to share our lives with other Christians, especially with those who need us.

There is SO MUCH that we women CAN and MUST do!

CONCLUSION: The foolish woman yearns for position outside her role or she feels that there really is nothing she can do because she is a woman. The wise woman finds the roles the Lord has given her challenging and rewarding. She rejoices in her lot.

DAILY BIBLE READINGS:
Sunday: Genesis 1:27; 2:22; 3:1-16; In the beginning.
Monday: 1 Corinthians 11:3; 1 Timothy 2:1-14, In the early church.
Tuesday: Ephesians 5:21-33, God's plan for husband and wife.
Wednesday: Proverbs 31:10-31, A worthy woman
Thursday: 1 Timothy 5:5-14, a worthy widow.
Friday: Proverbs 12:4; 19:13,14; Psalms 128:3, a good wife.
Saturday: Ruth, chapters 1-4, a love story.
MEMORY VERSE: Genesis 2:18

Chapter 7

The Wise Woman Knows
HER OPPORTUNITIES

"A wise man will make more opportunities than he finds," Sir Francis Bacon said. It would be interesting, with this statement in mind, to read biographies of successful people, as the world sees success. I would venture a guess that they made more opportunities than they found. They certainly were not like the man who missed his golden opportunity because he was at his neighbor's house complaining about his rotten luck.

Someone else has said, "Opportunity knocks but once." While this may not be true in every case, much of our success in the world and as Christians may depend on our ability to see and grasp opportunity when it comes. This is equally true in spiritual and secular matters.

Webster defines opportunity as: "Fit time; a favorable juncture of circumstances; a good chance."

Opportunity for what? We might ask ourselves. Are we seeking social position? Wealth? Fame? While a measure of each of these may come to a Christian, she must never forget that she is sanctified, consecrated--set apart for a special purpose. She will not sit idly waiting for a "favorable juncture of circumstances," but she will be wide awake, ready to seize every opportunity to do good. She will heed Paul's admonition:

> See then that ye walk circumspectly, not as fools, but as wise, Redeeming the time, because the days are evil. Wherefore be ye not unwise, but understanding what the will of the Lord is (Ephesians 5:5-17 KJ).

I. THE WISE USE, FOOLISH LOSE OPPORTUNITY. We find examples of both men and women in each category as we study God's word.

A. In warning his followers to be watchful for his second coming,

Jesus told the story of the wise and foolish virgins. According to Jewish custom, the ten were waiting while the bridegroom went to the home of the bride's father to get her. Five were wise because they took an extra supply of oil; perhaps they knew that delays often occurred. The other five were foolish; they took enough oil to last until midnight, which actually should have sufficed. But they had not prepared to "go the extra mile." Individual responsibility is stressed when the five wise pointed out that there might not be enough oil for any of them if they divided; the foolish simply would have to go to those who sold oil and buy for themselves. And we know the sad ending of the story, for them, when the bridegroom said, "I do not know you" (Matthew 25:1-13).

Some have suggested that the foolish virgins do not represent those outside Christ, for they were members of the wedding party. Apparently they represent those in the kingdom who want to do barely enough to be saved while staying as close to the world as possible. Maybe when they saw no real need to attend worship services on Sunday or Wednesday night, they were absent when friends whom they had invited to visit came. They did not return, though. They felt unwanted because their friend was not there to greet them. When those whom the wise woman had invited came, she was there to greet them and to introduce them to the minister and other members. She then made an opportunity to discuss with them what they had seen and heard and finally knew the joy of seeing them obey their Lord.

B. Through the ages Thomas has been remembered as "doubting Thomas" because he missed an opportunity to be with the other apostles on the night following Christ's resurrection. You remember that, although the doors were shut, Jesus appeared to them, saying, "Peace be with you." He showed them his hands and his side. He then breathed on them and said, "Receive the Holy Spirit."

Thomas missed seeing the Christ's proof that he, was, indeed, the risen Lord; he also missed the giving of the Holy Spirit. When he was told what had happened, he declared that he would not believe until he had seen. Eight days later he was there when the Lord appeared and had Thomas feel his hands and place his hand in his side.

Thomas cried, "My Lord and my God."

Jesus said to him, "Have you believed because you have seen me? Blessed are those who have not seen and yet believe" (John 20:19-25).

The foolish woman is just as sure to miss a blessing when she fails to assemble with the saints; indeed, she misses being with the Lord, for he has said he will be among them when as few as two or three are assembled in his name. Unless she is hindered by illness or circumstances beyond her control, the wise woman never misses the opportunity for spiritual growth afforded in meeting with her brothers and sisters in Christ to worship her Lord.

C. Wise women of Jesus' time followed and served him during his ministry. We are told in Luke 8 that, among those traveling with him, in addition to the twelve apostles, were women who had been healed, including Mary Magdalene, Joanna, and Susanna, and many others who were contributing from their private means for the support of Jesus and the apostles. They saw an opportunity for service to their master by their personal ministry and in the use of their money.

It has been said that faithful women were last at the cross, first at the tomb, and first to proclaim the resurrection. We find this is true, as we read that Mary Magdalene and the other Mary, the mother of Jesus were at the foot of the cross. The two Marys were up before dawn to anoint the body of Jesus (Matthew 28; Mark 16; John 20). They took every opportunity to be with the Lord.

II. THE WISE WOMAN MAKES THE MOST OF OPPORTUNITIES. She realizes that, at best, each family is a unit for a relatively short time. She takes time to work and play with her loved ones--to build memories that will sustain her as she becomes a "seasoned saint." She reaches out from her own family to her spiritual family and to the community.

A. "Honor your father and your mother, that your days may be prolonged in the land which the Lord your God gives you," was one of the original ten commandments (Exodus 20:12 NASV). When the Pharisees and scribes taunted Jesus because his disciples did not wash their hands before eating bread, he quoted this commandment and that in Exodus 21:17, "And he who curses his father or mother shall surely be put to death." By their traditions, he said, they were invalidating the word of God by claiming that anything of theirs by which their parents might have profited had been given to God.

If girls realized how quickly their days at home with their parents would pass, they would make opportunities to honor their parents both in obedience and in looking for ways to lighten burdens and make home life happy. Showing respect and care for parents does not cease, of course, when we leave home. But in our mobile society our chances to do for aging parents may be hampered by distance and time.

B. Brothers and sisters, too, may be surprised at the rapidity with which they are caught up in lives away from home. There are, surely, those times when they think a pesky little brother never will quit teasing. Then each goes his own way, and they will spend hundreds of dollars, drive thousands of miles just to spend a few days together. After Jacob and Esau were reconciled in their later years, they probably wished for the opportunity to go back and erase some of the jealousy troubling their young manhood.

We must seek the spiritual as well as the physical well being of our parents, brothers and sisters. I knew one woman who became a Christian after she was married. She wrote her brother and his wife, telling them of her new-found faith. Each time she wrote she enclosed a tract or quoted a scripture. They were older people when I knew them; the brother and his wife were faithful Christians, and he had been preaching the gospel for years. We don't read much about Andrew in the New Testament. In John 1 we learn that he was a disciple of John and that he heard John when he recognized Jesus as the Lamb of God. Andrew and his fellow disciple followed Jesus. The first person Andrew sought out to tell the good news that he had found the Christ was his own brother, Simon, whom he brought to Christ. Jesus immediately called him "Cephas" or ("Peter") and we hear much of and from Peter in the New Testament.

C. Women who have lost their husbands often warn other wives that they should make opportunities to be with and care for their husbands. One widow said, "It is as if you had lost half of yourself." Even—or perhaps especially-unbelieving husbands should be loved and treated with respect.

"Wife, how do you know whether you will save your husband?" Paul asks (1 Corinthians 7:16 RSV).

Peter tells us that the reverent and chaste behavior of wives may win a husband who will not hear the word (1 Peter 3:1,2). And especially blessed are we who have believing husbands, on whom we can lean spiritually. We should "do them good and not evil all the days of our lives." In fact, we should "notice him, regard him, honor him, prefer him, venerate and esteem him, defer to him, praise him, and love and admire him exceedingly" (Ephesians 5:33 Amp.).

Often we hear of couples who have been married seventy-five years or even more. They have had many opportunities to build a strong relationship, to show appreciation for each other. Others lose a companion at an early age, without warning. It is not at all uncommon to read of a man's death from a heart attack when he was in his forties or fifties, some even in their thirties. An old song warns, "He may leave you and never return." Certainly we are not saying that you should become a worrier, apprehensive of your husband's every sneeze or sniffle. But we are saying that wives must not neglect opportunities--yea, they should make opportunities--to be the good wife they would wish they had been if they lose him.

We are much more likely to think of things we wish he had done for us than of things he may have asked us to do for him. A button missing from a shirt is a small thing, but it can be a real threat to harmony in the home if he has to ask three times to get it sewed on. Of course he knows where the needles and thread are, but this is a small opportunity to show love and appreciation in a concrete way. Maybe he wanted you to attend a game or to make a visit with him but because you had not used your time wisely you were not available. Think of ways you can make the opportunity to be a good and loving wife.

D. "Lo, Children are an heritage of the Lord," the psalmist said in Psalms 127:3. Whether they are a blessing to their parents and the world is determined by their early training perhaps more than by their heredity. We have such a very few years to accomplish this awesome but rewarding task, that nothing should take precedence over it. As Helen Young has said so beautifully, "Houses can wait, dishes can wait, but children won't wait." You should weigh your priorities very carefully before deciding to spend time away from small children, or even teen-agers, that might be needed in their discipline and training. This is not to say you are to have no time for yourself; this may be necessary to help you to be a good parent. But you must use well the opportunity, respect the responsibility to train the child in the "nurture and admonition of the Lord" (Ephesians 6:4 KJ). Other translations say in the discipline and instruction of the Lord. We might even become so conscious of the problem of child abuse that we neglect necessary correction, even a sensible spanking when the situation demands it. Remember the wise man's warning:

"He who spares his rod hates his son,
But he who loves him disciplines him diligently" (Proverbs 13:24 NASV).

The best trained child surely is one whose parents can enjoy him. This means that we delight in his every accomplishment, whether it is taking his first step, saying his first word, or making his first home run in Little League. A little girl may indicate her desire for your attention and time by patting the floor beside her when she is still unable to talk. You can become a part of her make believe world simply by sitting and resting in a lawn chair while she imagines you two are traveling afar as she rides her tricycle in circles on the patio. When she becomes a teenager, she may not be so anxious to have you visit her school as she was in elementary school, but still you can find ways, make opportunities, to stay close to her while letting her begin to break the apron strings.

With the aid of capable Bible class teachers, a child should have his spiritual guidelines pretty well established before he leaves junior high school. While it may be hard to schedule, time must be made for instruction in the home, for Bible classes are simply to reinforce our own teaching, not to take its place. We must make the time at least to see that we and our children prepare their Bible class lessons. We must pray together. We dare not leave this responsibility to others. We cannot allow the child to decide for himself whether or not he will attend worship. We must help him study God's word. Remember:

"The rod of correction imparts wisdom, but a child left to itself disgraces his mother." (Proverbs 29:15 NIV)

E. As she has opportunity, the wise woman does good to all, especially to those who are of the household of faith.

Because we are brothers and sisters in Christ, we are especially aware of each other's needs, just as we are of our temporal family's. We should be ready to work under the direction of the elders or deacons and with our Bible classes or visitation groups. However, we need not wait for assignments from others. We may have the opportunity to speak a word of encouragement or to lend a helping hand just by being there at a moment when it is needed most. New Christians are in need especially of our help toward their spiritual growth. They may not understand some of the terms we have been familiar with all our lives. They may need our fellowship to assist them in weeding out old habits or to replace worldly friends who might impede their progress. In Galatians 6:1-10 Paul admonishes us to bear one another's burdens and "thus fulfill the law of Christ."

Like the widow worthy to be helped by the church, of whom we read in 1 Timothy 5:9 and 10, the wise woman has been willing not only to serve fellow Christians in menial ways, but she has relieved the distressed and has conscientiously done all the good she can. She sees opportunities to help the young mother just home from the hospital with a new baby or to take time to sit and visit or perhaps to go shopping with a woman recently widowed, whose husband always went with her to buy groceries.

When a new neighbor has moved in is a very opportune time to offer a cake, a pitcher of lemonade, or even baby sitting while the house is being put in order. This, too, is a good time to invite them to worship with you. You may even have the difficult task of helping them to fill spiritual needs of which they may not be aware.

The Shunammite woman, of whom we read in 2 Kings 4:8-10, made the opportunity to do good. She observed Elisha as he ministered in Shunem and invited him to eat with her and her husband. Realizing that he was a man of God and that he passed by frequently, she asked her husband to provide an upper room and furnish it so that he would feel free to stay with them. We know that she was rewarded for her hospitality. This generation of Christians seldom has the opportunity to have a visiting evangelist stay in its homes; we usually have them stay at a motel. Surely it is easier on the preacher, who can relax and come and go at will. But among our happiest memories and those which I'm sure helped us grow spiritually are the times when a man of God stayed in our home. Our schools of preaching may offer us an opportunity for this type of service as young preachers travel to seek support or employment. We can make lasting friendships and at the same time serve the Lord by opening our homes to fellow Christians attending workshops or helping with campaigns in our area.

The wise woman never forgets that in serving others she is serving the Lord. Remember, Jesus taught this truth forcefully in his picture of the judgment scene:

> Then the King will say to those on His right, "Come, you who are blessed of My Father, inherit the kingdom prepared for you from the foundation of the world. For I was hungry, and you gave Me something to eat; I was thirsty, and you gave Me drink; I was a stranger, and you invited Me in; naked, and you clothed Me; I was sick, and you visited Me; I was in prison, and you came to Me. . . . Truly I say to you, to the extent that you did it to one of these brothers of Mine, even the least of them, you did it to Me." (Matthew 25:34-36 NASV)

III. WISDOM DICTATES THAT A WOMAN MAKE OPPORTUNITY FOR SPIRITUAL GROWTH. She will grow spiritually as she encourages her family and others, but she must take time for her own study and meditation. Some of us may become so zealous for good works that we need to be warned that we are spreading ourselves too thin.

We simply must not try to live on a milk-diet, spiritually, all our lives. The writer of Hebrews lamented that the Christians to whom he was writing were too immature for some of the teaching he needed to give them. They were not ready for the meat of the word but needed to be taught again the first principles of God's word.

"For every one who lives on milk is unskilled in the word of righteousness, for he is a child. But solid food is for the mature, for those who have their faculties trained by practice to distinguish good from evil" (Hebrews 5:13,14 RSV).

IV. THE WISE WOMAN SEES THE DOORS OPEN TO HER. Perhaps a main reason we do not see these open doors is that we are not soul conscious. Do you really believe that those who are not in Christ are lost? Do you believe that those who teach as doctrine the commandments of men are lost? Paul said all spiritual blessings are in Christ (Ephesians 1:3). Jesus said, "In vain do they worship me, teaching as doctrines the precepts of men (Matthew 15:9 RSV).

You can not reach everyone who is lost, but there are some you can help to understand the word of God more perfectly. There are those who are becoming disillusioned with false doctrine and are seeking with good and honest hearts for the truth. There are ways for you to help them to understand and obey.

Many congregations are making available to their members names provided by the World Bible School, which is simply a tool for us to use in carrying out the great commission, to go into all the world. All you must do as teacher is to write a personal message to the student on the introduction lesson and mail it to each of your students. Then you supply a six lesson booklet and perhaps a New Testament and a certificate to those who complete the course. Information is supplied so that those who wish to be baptized into Christ are put in contact with missionaries or teams doing follow up work. Thousands are being taught in this way.

Bible class teachers have a wonderful opportunity to reach beyond those actually enrolled. Many children being brought to class in busses have parents who may become interested when they see the results in their childrens' lives.

Doors are opened by benevolence. Most churches maintain food and clothing rooms, where volunteers are needed to supply both physical and spiritual needs of those who come for help.

Hospitality opens many doors. With better homes than ever before, are we using them for the Lord as generously as our mothers and fathers did? Do we hear a sincere, "Come over to our house" as often as it once was heard?

Sympathy is a door opener. Bereavement brings into a home relatives and friends from afar. There is need for food and shelter. As you supply those needs, you are doing it for the Lord, and He is doing it for them. Hearts are more open, and you may be led to someone hungering for the truth which you can supply through tracts, Bible correspondence courses, or personal study.

CONCLUSION: The foolish woman finds doors of opportunity closed because she procrastinates or simply fails to see them.

The wise woman sees and makes opportunities; she makes the most of them. She is a blessing to her family, friends, and community. Because of her good works others praise the Lord.

DAILY BIBLE READINGS:
Sunday: Matthew 25:1-13, The wise and foolish virgins.
Monday: John 20:19-24, He missed a meeting...and the Lord.
Tuesday: 2 Kings 4:8-37, It is well.
Wednesday: Romans 15:1-7, Please your neighbor for his good.
Thursday: Mark 14:3-9; Luke 7:37-48, Her good deed made her immortal.
Friday: Matthew 25:14-30, Opportunity neglected.
Saturday: Matthew 25:31-46, Serving the Lord through others.
MEMORY VERSE: Ephesians 5:15,16.

Chapter 8

The Wise Woman Knows
FREEDOM

Never having been a slave, we may not appreciate fully the pent up emotion behind the words uttered by a black woman who has saved for years to buy her freedom: "I'm FREE!" Or that of the black man who has been given his liberty: "I'm a freed man!"

Goethe said, "None are more hopelessly enslaved than those who falsely believe they are free."

You've never been a slave? Think a minute. If you reached the age of accountability--which you surely did before you became a Christian--you WERE enslaved. You were shackled by the deepest bondage to which one ever has been subjected: SIN.

Not having been possessed of seven devils, as is said of Mary Magdalene, we may not feel the lifting of a tremendous load, as she apparently did. And we may not show the overwhelming gratitude that prompted her to devote her life and her wealth to her Lord.

Men and women have fought and died for civil liberty. God's word points the way to man's greatest freedom...freedom from sin. Like civil liberty, this also is costly. It requires the complete surrender of our lives to Christ. Yet the new life is worth any sacrifice, its rewards everlasting.

I. CHRIST IS THE LIBERATOR. Every one who is accountable is a slave, therefore in need of salvation: "All have sinned and fall short of the glory of God (Romans 3:23).

A. Every one who commits sin is a slave. The foolish woman may be like the proud Jews who were incensed when Jesus told them, "You shall know the truth and the truth shall make you free" (John 8:32). Since they were Abraham's seed and had never been in physical bondage, they simply could not understand that they had any need for liberation. She may have grown up in a religious family, may even have been sprinkled when she was a baby. What she fails to realize is that each of us is responsible, individually, to know and obey the will of God.

"He who is of God hears the words of God," Jesus told the Jews.

That word is like a mirror, convicting one with a good and honest heart of her sin. She becomes conscious of her enslavement, remembering Jesus' words, "Truly, truly, I say to you, every one who commits sin is a slave to sin (John 8:34 RSV).

The foolish woman may persist, as did the Jews who tried to stone Jesus, in failure to recognize her need for salvation. After all, isn't she as good as some church members she knows? She goes to church on occasion--at Christmas and Easter, or perhaps when religious friends are visiting her. She pays her debts; she does not cheat and lie. The words she refuses to hear, though, caution that to know to do good and fail to do it is sin (James 4:17). If she would just open her Bible, she could see that even a just man like Cornelius needed to hear the gospel, the truth; that he was commanded to be baptized. This put him in Christ, where he had access to all spiritual blessings (Acts 10; Ephesians 1:3). Those who refuse to become Christians remain in the category of the wicked: "His own iniquities will capture the wicked, And he will be held with the cords of sin" (Proverbs 5:22 NASV).

When one who has failed to obey hears the word of God, she may experience the inward turmoil expressed so well by Paul:

> I find then the principle that evil is present in me, the one who wishes to do good. For I joyfully concur with the law of God in the inner man, but I see a different law in the members of my body, waging war against the law of my mind, and making me a prisoner of the law of sin which is in my members. Wretched man that I am! Who will set me free from the body of this death? (Romans 7:21-24 NASV)

She is taking the first faltering steps toward freedom! She is on her way to becoming a wise woman.

B. SIN LOSES ITS POWER FOR THOSE IN CHRIST. The dismal picture painted by Paul in the above passage changes as dramatically as does the landscape when the sun breaks through a cloud after a thunderstorm, when he exclaims: "There is therefore now no condemnation for those who are in Christ Jesus. For the law of the Spirit of life in Christ Jesus has set me free from the law of sin and death" (Romans 8:1, 2 RSV).

Just what happened, though, to change the picture? How does a rebellious or negligent foolish woman become an obedient, wise woman? How has she escaped condemnation? She is in Christ Jesus! What is this law of the Spirit of life which has set her free from the law of sin and death?

Either with the loving guidance of an understanding teacher, or perhaps through her own reading of the scriptures she has seen plainly from examples recorded in Acts that she must obey the gospel to become a Christian. Her reading of the four gospels has convinced her that Jesus is, truly, the son of God. She readily confesses her belief in him. Like the believing, convicted Jews on the day of Pentecost, she realized that she had been enslaved in sin. She cried out, "What shall I do?"

She then heard the answer given so many times to pentitent believers, in the words of Peter, "Repent and be baptized every one of you in the name of Jesus Christ for the forgiveness of your sins; and you shall receive the gift of the Holy Spirit."

She did not then have to seek out and join a denomination; the Lord added her to his church (Acts 2:47). Since the church is Christ's body, (Ephesians 1:22,23), she is in Christ. She was baptized into him: "For as many of you as have been baptized into Christ have put on Christ" (Galatians 3:27 KJ).

She is no longer a slave to sin. She is a joyful slave to righteousness:

> Don't you know that when you offer yourselves to someone to obey him as slaves, you are slaves to the one whom you obey--whether you are slaves to sin, which leads to death, or to obedience, which leads to righteousness? But thanks be to God that, though you used to be slaves to sin, you wholeheartedly obeyed the form of teaching to which you were entrusted. You have been set free from sin and have become slaves to righteousness (Romans 6:16-18 NIV).

The once foolish woman has become a new person, a truly wise woman. She is enjoying life at its fullest. This is living! Earlier in the chapter quoted above, Paul describes the transformation:

> Do you not know that all of us who have been baptized into Christ Jesus were baptized into his death? We were buried therefore with him by baptism into death, so that as Christ was raised from the dead by the glory of the Father, we too might walk in newness of life...We know that our old self was crucified with him so that the sinful body might be destroyed,

and we might no longer be enslaved to sin...So you also must consider yourselves dead to sin and alive to God in Christ Jesus (Romans 6:3,4,6,11 RSV).

C. IT IS CHRIST WHO HAS GIVEN HER FREEDOM, which is freedom indeed! He wants those whom he has freed to remain free. During the early days of the church, it was necessary for Paul and others to remind Christians that they were no longer under the old law. In the closing verses of Galatians four, he compares the old law to Hagar, the slave woman; those in Christ to children of the free woman. He concludes, "It is for freedom that Christ has set us free. Stand firm, then, and do not let yourselves be burdened again by a yoke of slavery" (Galatians 5:1 NASV).

After having warned the Jews that every one who commits sin is a slave to sin, Christ declared: "The slave does not continue in the house for ever; the son continues for ever. So if the Son makes you free, you will be free indeed" (John 8:35,36 RSV).

Having been born into the body of Christ, the woman once enslaved by sin is freed by him from her old life. She is really free at last!

D. She is now freed from guilt. Her sins have been washed away. You will remember that Paul was told by Ananias to arise, be baptized, and wash away his sins (Acts 22:16).

When God forgives sin, he wipes the slate clean. Someone has said that a sinner prayed for forgiveness; he had repented of his sin. God forgave him. Conscience stricken, the sinner implored again, "Please, Father, forgive that sin." God replied, "WHAT sin?"

Does this mean that one does not have to bear the consequence of his forgiven sin? Suppose a woman has been sentenced to imprisonment for murdering her husband. Among her visitors is another woman who loves souls, even those convicted of murder. The prisoner hears the gospel, believes and obeys it. She is a new creature in Christ, a saint behind prison walls. The state still requires that she serve out her term, at least until she can be paroled. But she actually is free . . . free from the guilt of her sin.

Her greatest problem may be in forgiving herself as God has forgiven her. Her teacher may turn with her to the book of Hebrews, where the new law is again being shown superior to the old. They read:

The blood of goats and bulls and the ashes of a heifer sprinkled on those who are ceremonially unclean sanctify them so that they are outwardly clean. How much more, then, will the blood of Christ, who through the eternal Spirit offered himself unblemished to God, cleanse our consciences from acts that lead to death, so that we may serve the living God! (Hebrews 8:13-14 NASV).

"How can I remain free from sin?" the new Christian may ask. "In here I must associate with sinners every day. It is not going to be easy for me to break my old habits, to really be a new person."

What a joy it is for her sister in Christ to turn with her again to God's word and read: "God is light; in him there is no darkness at all. If we claim to have fellowship with him yet walk in darkness, we lie and do not live by the truth. But if we walk in the light, as he is in the light, we have fellowship with one another, and the blood of Jesus, his Son, purifies us from every sin" (1 John 1:5-7 NIV).

They note that this cleansing is a continuing process, encouraged by the fellowship of Christians, which can be provided while she is in prison and when she is released.

E. She is to be free of worry. God has promised that those who put his kingdom first will have the necessities of life. Those who let their concern for material things occupy their prime interest are classified with the heathens, who have no faith. In the sermon on the mount, Jesus warned that one can not serve God and mammon. He concludes:

> Therefore I say unto you, Take no thought for your life, what you shall eat, or what ye shall drink; nor yet for your body, what ye shall put on. Is not the life more than meat, and the body than raiment? ...Therefore take no thought, saying, What shall we eat? or, What shall we drink? or, Wherewithal shall we be clothed? (For after all these things do the Gentiles seek:) for your heavenly Father knoweth that ye have need of all these things. But seek ye first the kingdom of God, and his righteousness; and all these things shall be added unto you. Take therefore no thought for the morrow: for the morrow shall take thought for the things of itself. Sufficent unto the day is the evil thereof (Matthew 6:25, 31-34 KJ).

Does this mean that a Christian is to make no effort to meet the needs of his family? It does not. It does mean that we are not to let these material things take precedence over the spiritual. Paul teaches very plainly that a person should work and that he should support his family: "If any will not work, let him not eat. For we hear that some of you are living in idleness, mere busybodies, not doing any work. Now such persons we command and exhort in the Lord Jesus Christ to do their work in quietness and to earn their own living" (2 Thessalonians 3:10-12 RSV).

Actually, one may nullify his faith by failing to provide for his family: "If anyone does not provide for his relatives, and especially for his immediate family, he has denied the faith and is worse than an unbeliever" (1 Timothy 5:8 NIV).

Still, we are commanded not to be anxious, to worry; one who truly trusts in the providence of God will be freed from these. Paul wrote the Philippians: "Be careful for nothing; but in every thing by prayer and supplication with thanksgiving let your requests be made known unto God. And the peace of God, which passeth all understanding, shall keep your hearts and minds through Christ Jesus (Philippians 4:6,7 KJ).

In other words, as a Christian we are to do our best, tell God about our needs and concerns, trust in his providence. Then we will have peace of mind. We are not to fret over what is past, that of which we have received forgiveness. We are not to borrow trouble from tomorrow. We are to live to the best of our ability a day at a time, whatever our outward circumstances.

Peter says, "Cast all your anxieties on him, for he cares about you" (1 Peter 5:7 RSV).

Isn't it great to realize that God takes a personal interest in your well being? Jude tells us in verse 24 that God, through Jesus Christ, is able to keep us from falling and to present us before his glorious presence without fault and with great joy. Paul prayed that the Ephesians might be strengthened with might through his Spirit in the inner man. God's ability to work through us is really beyond our comprehension: "Now to him who by the power at work within us is able to do far more abundantly than all that we ask or think" (Ephesians 3:16,20 RSV). How, then, can we worry?

II. THE WISE WOMAN USES FREEDOM WELL. Having been set free by the Son does not mean we are "free to do our own thing." While early Christians were caught up in the struggle between the keeping of the old law and their new-found freedom in Christ, we can be subject to just as great a struggle in overcoming the immoral climate in our society. The advice given by Paul to the Galatians can be just as meaningful to us:

> For you were called to freedom, brethren; only do not use your freedom as an opportunity for the flesh, but through love be servants of one another. For the whole law is fulfilled in one

word, "You shall love your neighbor as yourself." But if you bite and devour one another take heed that you are not consumed by one another. But I say, walk by the Spirit, and do not gratify the desires of the flesh. For the desires of the flesh are against the Spirit, and the desires of the Spirit are against the flesh; for these are opposed to each other, to prevent you from doing what you would. But if you are led by the Spirit you are not under the law (Galatians 5:13-18 RSV).

Your life can not be a vacuum; it is not possible for you to live a life pleasing to God just by failing to do wrong...actually by being good for nothing! Remember the passage we studied above, that you have been "set free from sin and have become slaves of righteousness." In Galatians 5:21 Paul listed the works of the flesh, from which the one who walks by the Spirit is to be free. Then he listed the fruits of the Spirit, "Love, joy, peace, patience, kindness, goodness, faithfulness, gentleness, and self control" (Galatians 5:22,23). These qualities will be manifest in the life of one who has become a slave to righteousness.

Peter admonished, "Live as free men, yet without using your freedom as a pretext for evil; but live as servants of God. Honor all men. Love the brotherhood. Fear God. Honor the emperor." (1 Peter 2:16,17 RSV).

Christ, himself, set us an example of obedience and service to God. He said he came not to be served but to serve. Here, again, we might recall that he taught that in serving others we serve him. He taught respect for others and emphasized the necessity of loving the brotherhood as a testimony to the world of true discipleship. His new commandment was "that you love one another; even as I have loved you, that you also love one another" (John 13:34). He said, "Render therefore unto Caesar the things that are Caesar's, and to God the things that are God's" (Matthew 21:21 RSV). The righteous life is a balanced life, a life of freedom. One is free to do as he pleases, but his will is subject to that of the Father; therefore he is pleased to be an obedient servant of his Lord.

III. HER EARTHLY FREEDOM IS A FORETASTE OF GLORY. Although she has become a servant of righteousness, the wise woman has become a member of the household of God and enjoys its privileges as a child, not a slave. With this new relationship comes the responsibility to behave like a member of the family, to shun the temptations of the old life, which would bring dishonor on the household and death to the sinner. Paul explains this:

We have an obligation--but it is not to the sinful nature, to live according to it. For if you live according to the sinful nature, you will die; but if by the Spirit you put to death the misdeeds of the body, you will live, because those who are led by the Spirit of God are sons of God. For you did not receive a spirit that makes you a slave again to fear, but you received the Spirit of sonship. And by him we cry, "*Abba*, Father." The Spirit himself testifies with our spirit that we are God's children. Now if we are children, then we are heirs--heirs of God and co-heirs with Christ, if indeed we share in his suffering in order that we may also share in his glory (Romans 8:12-17 NIV).

A child experiences not only the joys of family life but also its sorrow and suffering. As she grows, she reflects the values inherent in her family. She has developed ideals and character which enable her to handle the freedom accorded her as she matures. It is a developmental process as she becomes more and more like her mother who is her ideal.

As we exercise our freedom in Christ, we become more like him. As we live in the Spirit, we walk with Christ: "Now the Lord is the Spirit, and where the Spirit of the Lord is, there is freedom. And we all, with unveiled faces beholding the glory of the Lord, are being changed into his likeness from one degree of glory to another; for this comes from the Lord who is the Spirit" (2 Corinthians 3:17,18 RSV).

IV. IT LEADS TO ETERNAL LIFE. The Christian woman may look back with regret, even shame, on her old way of life. But as she walks confidently in the new and living way, enjoying the fellowship of God's children, she does not dwell on the past but looks forward to the future--to eternal life.

She looks with regret at her friends, perhaps members of her own family, who still are enslaved to unrighteousness. They may consider themselves free--free to do as they please. But many who live by this philosophy are slaves to alcohol, drugs, perversion, vice of every kind. They may be bound by the love of money, literally selling their own souls for a few more dollars, which they can not take with them when their earthly life is ended. While those who live by the flesh are trying to pull the Christian back into their ways, she is working just as hard to lead them to THE Way, to Christ who can set them free.

Those who listen will, with her, reap a glorious reward; those who continue in sin will also receive their reward:

> When you were slaves to sin, you were free from the control of righteousness. What benefit did you reap at that time from the things you are now ashamed of? Those things result in death! But now that you have been set free from sin and have become slaves to God, the benefit you reap leads to holiness, and the result is eternal life. For the wages of sin is death, but the gift of God is eternal life in Christ Jesus our Lord (Romans 6:20-23 NIV).

CONCLUSION: The foolish woman persists in "doing her own thing" and finds herself enslaved to carnal pursuits which lead to spiritual death. She forfeits her right to true freedom. The wise woman knows Jesus Christ as Lord and master and gladly surrenders her will to his. She knows freedom from sin, guilt, and anxiety. Her reward will be eternal life, free from sorrow and pain.

DAILY BIBLE READING:
Sunday: Romans 7:7-25, A spiritual battle
Monday: Romans 6:1-18, Newness of life
Tuesday: Romans 8:1-39, More than conquerors
Wednesday: Hebrews 9:1-28, To serve the living God
Thursday: 1 John 1:1-10, Walking in the light
Friday: Luke 12:1-34, Do not be afraid
Saturday: 2 Corinthians 3:7-18; Romans 6:19-23, A foretaste of glory

MEMORY VERSES:
Romans 3:23, All have sinned
John 8:35,36, Free indeed

Chapter 9

The Wise Woman Knows
HAPPINESS

"Life, liberty, and the pursuit of happiness" are blessings our founding fathers attempted to secure for every American citizen in framing the constitution of the United States.

Many who came to these shores had seen others forfeit their lives for conscience's sake. They may actually have been fearful of their own lives. Here they sought protection from oppression, life free from fear.

Life alone, though, was not enough. To be meaningful, the new life must afford the liberty to act according to individual conscience, with no interference with freedom of speech or action, within the law, from the federal government.

This new life was to provide each individual the opportunity for the pursuit of happiness. Note that the framers of the constitution recognized that it was not the function of the government to assure happiness to each citizen. The plan was that each individual should be able to assume the responsibility for his own happiness, to pursue, seek after happiness in the ways that would fulfill his personal needs. The idea of pursuit suggests that happiness is having goals conducive to well being and mapping actions leading progressively to those goals.

In our studies we have learned that true happiness is in Christ Jesus. The wise woman recognizes that she can not find a fulfilled life outside the Lord's family, his church. She remembers that all spiritual blessings are IN Christ Jesus (Ephesians 1:3). When the foolish woman realizes that there is something lacking in her life, she can be led through the word to completeness in Christ, cautioned to avoid false teachers:

> See to it that no one takes you captive through hollow and deceptive philosophy, which depends on human tradition and

the basic principles of this world rather than on Christ. For in Christ all the fullness of the Deity lives in bodily form, and you have been given fullness in Christ, who is the head over every power and authority (Colossians 2:8-10 NIV).

One seeking completeness in Christ must realize, though, that happiness in Christ does not mean that her life will be free from pain and sorrow. Actually, you may have reached fullness in Christ when you can count suffering for his sake a privilege. Paul told Christians at Philippi: "You are given, in this battle, the privilege not merely of believing in Christ but also of suffering for his sake. It is now your turn to take part in that battle you once saw me engaged in, and which, in point of fact, I am still fighting" (Philippians 1:29-30 P).

I. THE WISE WOMAN IS A HAPPY WOMAN. Through knowledge and experience, she has found wisdom--through knowledge of God's word and exercise in righteousness.

A. Did you ever feel that you would be happy if you had a million dollars, or at least if you had a great deal more money that you had at the time? People have sacrificed their health in the pursuit of wealth then have found they were not so happy as they were just in earning an honest living. That wealth does not satisfy is demonstrated by suicides of those who have reached the top, financally, but have reached an unbearable low in personal relations. This should come as no surprise to those who listen to the wise man of old:

Happy is the man that findeth wisdom,
And the man that getteth understanding.
For the gaining of it is better than the gaining of silver,
And the profit thereof than fine gold.
She is more precious than rubies:
And none of the things thou canst desire are to be compared unto her (Proverbs 3:13-15 ASV).

Certainly the one who is wise will not take her own life. Because of her wisdom in becoming aware of the physical needs of her body, she may actually prolong her life. She will not become a faddist, but she will evaluate intelligently all that she reads on health and fitness. She will find out for herself what foods constitute good nutrition for herself and her family. She will be aware that even doctors may change their minds about what is good to keep the human mechanism running smoothly. She certainly will have the fortitude to avoid those things detrimental to health, such as drugs, alcohol, tobacco, even unhealthful treats.

B. The wise woman may become a leader in her field, gaining riches and honor from her profession. You can name women who applied themselves to learning about health and nutrition who are being paid well to demonstrate proper cooking methods on television. Solomon said, of wisdom, "Length of days is in her right hand; In her left hand are riches and honor" (Proverbs 3:16 ASV).

C. Wisdom's way is pleasant. Don't you feel good when you have done what you know is right? You were really tempted to buy that fashionable outift, but you realized it would put a strain on the clothing budget. Besides, one of the children needed new shoes, and it would be nice to be able to buy a new suit for your husband while it is on sale. If you had bought the outfit for yourself, you probably would have had in the pit of the stomach guilt feelings while you opened cans and prepared a hasty dinner. Since you resisted the temptation, you hum a tune while you prepare your family's favorite meal. (Maybe that dress and accessories will go on sale, and you can buy them with the money your grateful husband set aside for your birthday!)

Wisdom's way has led to an evening of pleasant family fellowship. There is no wrangling over which bills to pay and which can be stalled for a week or so. Your peaceful household settles down happily for the evening's devotional. Solomon knew: "Her ways are ways of pleasantness, And all her paths are peace (Proverbs 3:17 ASV).

Eve ate of the tree of knowledge of good and evil, which had been forbidden to her, and was banished from the garden so that she could not eat of the tree of life in its midst. Those who persist in the way of wisdom will eventually be allowed to partake of the tree of life (Revelations 2:7). In overcoming trials and temptations, they will have demonstrated their wisdom: "She (wisdom) is a tree of life to them that lay hold upon her: And happy is every one that retaineth her" (Proverbs 3:18 ASV).

II. THE ROAD TO HAPPINESS MAY LEAD THROUGH A VALE OF TEARS. Suffering for wrong doing or neglect is not on that road, however. But one who suffers for righteousness is blessed, or happy. Evangelists who had been imprisoned and beaten because they preached Jesus rejoiced that they were counted worthy to suffer shame and dishonor for his name (Acts 5:40-41). They assured those persecuting them that they were determined to obey

God, rather than man. They continued to teach and preach Jesus as the Christ daily in the temple and at home.

A. Are your children happy when you correct them? Are you happy when your husband, or perhaps an elder, finds it necessary to reprove you? If so, you are a very mature person. Our children can not be expected to understand that we correct them because we want them to become a well adjusted, happy person, pleasing to God. We must explain this to them and always show that we love them, even when we must reprove. Christ died for us when we were yet sinners. God loves us even when we sin. He would not be a just, loving God if he did not, through his word, correct us when we are astray. Just as we discipline our children because we love them, God so disciplines, teaches us.

One of Job's friends counseled, "Behold, how happy is the man whom God reproves, So do not despise the discipline of the Almighty" (Job 5:17 NASV).

B. You may ask, "Would I expect to suffer hardship in Christ, where all spiritual blessings are?"

Let's turn to God's word for the answer:

"My son, do not make light of the Lord's discipline,
and do not lose heart when he rebukes you,
because the Lord disciplines those he loves,
and he punishes everyone he accepts as sons."

Endure hardship as discipline; God is treating you as sons. For what son is not disciplined by his father? If you are not disciplined (and everyone undergoes discipline), then you are illegitimate children and not true sons. Moreover, we have all had human fathers who disciplined us and we respected them for it. How much more should we submit to the Father of our spirits and live! Our fathers disciplined us for a little while as they thought best; but God disciplines us for our good, that we may share in his holiness. No discipline seems pleasant at the time, but painful. Later on, however, it produces a harvest of righteousness and peace for those who have been trained by it (Hebrews 12:5-11 NIV).

C. We share in Christ's suffering so that we may partake of his glory. Why should we expect to escape suffering when the son of God suffered and died for us? Jesus "offered up prayers and petitions with loud cries and tears to the one who could save him from death, and he was heard because of his reverent submission.

Although he was a son, he learned obedience from what he suffered" (Hebrews 5:7,8 NIV).

If we are unwilling to suffer with Christ, we are forfeiting our right, as children of God, fellow heirs with Christ, to share in Christ's glory. In our earthly families, we share happiness and sorrow, honor and dishonor. It is a heart breaking experience to visit with a family when one of its members has been arrested or expelled from school. Yet as mature Christians we must comfort the distressed, however painful it may be for them and for us. But what a joy it is to visit--perhaps with the same family--when one of the members has been honored for outstanding accomplishment. It is the same in God's family: "We are children of God, and if children, then heirs, heirs of God and fellow heirs with Christ, provided we suffer with him in order that we may also be glorified with him" (Romans 8:16b-17 RSV).

Suffering with Christ is being identified with him, enjoying his blessing while experiencing persecution or ridicule because we are his; we live the principles he taught, even when they put us at odds with our associates in school, in business, yes, even in the home. Our happiness is then produced by a clear conscience.

Our happiness is derived from the knowledge that, though all the world forsake us, Jesus is with us. After giving the "great commission" he promised his followers, "I am with you always, even unto the end of the world" (Matthew 28:20 KJ).

Peter points out that such suffering is common to Christians throughout the world. Somehow, knowing that we are not the only ones who are tempted by Satan and must resist the ways of the world, brings comfort to the believer. But the greatest consolation is knowing that God cares about us and that he will participate in our relief from suffering: "And after you have suffered a little while, the God of all grace, who has called you to his eternal glory in Christ, will himself restore, establish, and strengthen you" (1 Peter 5:10 RSV).

III. CHRIST GAVE A VIVID PICTURE OF TRUE HAPPINESS. This is not happiness as the world sees it, in the exaltation of self, the acquisition of things, position or power. Rather, it is the emptying of self, the losing of selfish motives. Someone has said that Christ's teaching in the sermon on the mount is that "the way up is down." It is "less of self and more of thee" expressed so beautifully in song.

At the beginning of the "sermon on the mount," Jesus draws a series of verbal pictures of true happiness. We call them the beatitudes. Each starts with the word *blessed*, which can be, and is, translated *happy*. (Matthew 5:3-11 RSV).

A. Happiness is realizing our dependence on God: "Blessed are the poor in spirit, for theirs is the kingdom of heaven." Certainly this is not being poor in worldly possessions or money. It is not in having a poor image of self. It is simply realizing our spiritual need, our need for God's providential care. Realizing your need, you are willing to obey Christ, to submit your will to his. When you are baptized into Christ, you enter his kingdom; the kingdom is (*present tense*) yours. We all look forward to God's everlasting kingdom, but we must understand that the kingdom and church are one; therefore we enter the kingdom when we are added to the church and enjoy its blessings in this life.

B. Happiness is translating sorrow into rejoicing: "Blessed are those who mourn, for they shall be comforted." The foolish woman says, "Oh, no!" When one mourns, she is unhappy! I'll 'get my gusto' while I can." To her, happiness is having fun, avoiding pain, sorrow, or vexation. The Christian can realize comfort even in the loss of a loved one through her faith in Christ and his promise of resurrection. But this is not the primary thrust of this beatitude. This mourning is the godly sorrow which leads to repentance, to restoration to God's favor. Paul describes this mourning:

> For even if I made you sorry with my letter, I do not regret it (though I did regret it), for I see that that letter grieved you, though only for a while. As it is, I rejoice, not because you were grieved, but because you were grieved into repenting; for you felt a godly grief, so that you suffered no loss through us. For godly grief produces a repentance that leads to salvation and brings no regret, but worldly grief produces death. For see what earnestness this godly grief has produced in you, what eagerness to clear yourselves, what indignation, what alarm, what longing, what zeal, what punishment! At every point you have proved yourselves guiltless in the matter. So although I wrote to you, it was not on account of the one who did the wrong, nor on account of the one who suffered the wrong, but in order that your zeal for us might be revealed to you in the sight of God. Therefore we are comforted (2 Corinthians 7:8-13 RSV).

The godly sorrow which leads to repentance produces a cleansed life, one at peace with God. This is comfort indeed.

C. Happiness is "letting go and letting God." "Blessed are the meek, for they shall inherit the earth." Meekness is not lack of spirit or temper. It may be described as power under control. Moses was described as meek, but this was said of him after his impetuous spirit had been disciplined by years of communion with God during wilderness wandering (Numbers 12:3). Jesus described himself as "meek and lowly in heart" (Matthew 11:29). This certainly did not mean that he was powerless, but that because of his willingness to be submissive to his father's will, he had the power to comfort the heavy laden, to give them rest. Meekness is listed as an attribute of God's chosen people, along with compassion, kindness, lowliness, and patience (Colossians 3:12). A meek and quiet spirit describes the personality which is precious in the sight of God (1 Peter 3:3,4).

How shall the meek inherit the earth? Those who crucify self in Christ, that is become members of his body, the church, are thereby children of God. We learned in Romans 8:16 and 17 (quoted above) that we are thus fellow heirs with Christ, heirs of God. Normally, children inherit the possessions of their father; this is true, also, in the spiritual realm. All the earth belongs to the Lord (Psalms 24:1). As children of God, thus under his control, the meek truly shall inherit the earth.

D. Happiness is a right relationship to God. "Blessed are those who hunger and thirst for righteousness, for they shall be satisfied." The person here described does not take a casual attitude toward the righteous life. Peter admonished those who had become obedient to the truth to long for "the sincere milk of the word," as babies long for milk. Your baby lets you know she is really hungry in the most effective manner she knows, screaming and crying. We who have been reared in an affluent society may have forgotten this urgent yearning for food.If we have never walked a dusty road without water, we may not remember how desperately one may long for a drink to assuage a compelling thirst. One who is motivated by such strong desire knows what is meant by hungering and thirsting *for righteousness*. He will give up anything else to obtain that state. To be crucified with Christ is to do just that! Christ compared the kingdom of heaven to a field containing a buried treasure. One who found the treasure went and sold all he had and purchased the field.

From Paul's writing to the Philippians, we learn that the fruits of righteousness come through Jesus Christ, that one who is filled with those fruits abounds in love, knowledge, and discernment, is pure and blameless:

> And it is my prayer that your love may abound more and more, with knowledge and all discernment, so that you may approve what is excellent, and may be pure and blameless for the day of Christ, filled with the fruits of righteousness which come through Jesus Christ, to the glory and praise of God (Philippians 1:9-11 RSV).

Since these righteous fruits come through Jesus Christ, they are available only to those who are in Christ. Certainly, then, one hungering and thirsting for righteousness will listen gladly to the gospel of Christ; having gained knowledge of Christ's sacrifice and his plan for salvation, he will be baptized into Christ (Galatians 3:27) and will "renounce irreligion and worldly passions, and live sober, upright, and godly...in this present world" (Titus 2:12 RSV).

E. Happiness is compassion for others, literally "feeling with" them. "Blessed are the merciful, for they shall obtain mercy." Mercy is more that pity; it is said to be the outward manifestation of pity. One commentator has said that in its strictest sense, it is forgiveness. A righteous person will be merciful as God is merciful:

> Jesus said, "But I tell you who hear me: love your enemies, do good to those who hate you, bless those who curse you, pray for those who mistreat you. If someone strikes you on one cheek, turn to him the other also. If someone takes your cloak, do not stop him from taking your tunic. Give to everyone who asks you, and if anyone takes what belongs to you, do not demand it back. Do to others as you would have them do to you...Then your reward will be great, and you will be sons of the Most High, because he is kind to the ungrateful and wicked. Be merciful, just as your Father is merciful"(Luke 6:27-31, 35b-36 NIV).

One who loves the soul of an enemy will be willing to forgive him. This forgiveness will be manifest in doing good to the hateful, blessing the one who curses, praying for the evildoer. In doing these things, we are manifesting godly attributes, thus are acting like children of God. We will be worthy recipients of his mercy.

F. Happiness is being able to see God: "Blessed are the pure in heart, for they shall see God." We understand that this purity of heart is not a mere muscle which is without disease, therefore able to pump blood through the system. It is the very center of man's being; its attitude determines his character. Jesus said, "How can you who are evil say anything good? For out of the overflow of the heart the mouth speaks. The good man brings good things out of the good stored up in him, and the evil man brings evil things out of the evil stored up in him (Matthew 12:34-35 NIV)."

From this we are not to conclude that the evil heart can not be purified; this is precisely what salvation is all about. Peter makes it very plain when he writes, "Having purified your souls by your obedience to the truth...You have been born anew...So put away all malice and all guile and insincerity and envy and all slander, like newborn babes, long for the pure spiritual milk, that by it you may grow up to salvation" (1 Peter 1:22,23; 2:1-2 RSV).

As one thus cleansed grows, he is spiritually inclined and can perceive things of the spirit...he can *see* God:

> But the natural man receiveth not the things of the Spirit of God: for they are foolishness unto him: neither can he know them, because they are spiritually discerned. But he that is spiritual judgeth all things, yet he himself is judged of no man. For who hath known the mind of the Lord, that he may instruct him? **But we have the mind of Christ (1 Corinthians 2:14-16 KJ).**

G. Happiness is sharing God's peace. "Blessed are the peacemakers, for they shall be called sons of God." The peace of God is more than settling quarrels between individuals or nations; one whose whole being is in accord with divine instruction has "peace that passes understanding" (Philippians 4:7). The task of the peacemaker, then, is to bring others into this relationship with God.

Peace is Christ's legacy: "Peace I leave with you; my peace I give you. I do not give to you as the world gives. Do not let your hearts be troubled and do not be afraid" (John 14:27 NIV). Paul said, "He is our peace" (Ephesians 2:14). Through his sacrifice, Christ made possible this peace:

> For God was pleased to have all his fullness dwell in him, and through him to reconcile to himself all things, whether things on earth or things in heaven, by making peace through his blood, shed on the cross (Colossians 1:19,20 NIV).

The peacemaker teaches others that the blood of Christ cleanses from sin, that in Christ they can find all spiritual blessings (1 John

1:7; Ephesians 1:3). By his righteous life he is recognized as a child of God: "By this the children of God and the children of the devil are obvious: any one who does not practice righteousness is not of God, nor the one who does not love his brother" (1 John 3:10 NASV).

H. Happiness is being persecuted with Christ. "Blessed are those who are persecuted for righteousness' sake, for theirs is the kingdom of heaven. Blessed are you when men revile you and persecute you and utter all kinds of evil against you falsely on my account. Rejoice and be glad, for your reward is great in heaven, for so men persecuted the prophets who were before you" (Matthew 5:10-11 RSV).

Our study of the "privilege" of suffering with Christ should help us understand this beatitude. We must remember, though, that this happiness comes from being persecuted *for righteousness' sake*. It is not blessed to suffer as an evildoer...for our own perversity. Much persecution comes when the life of Christ, reflected in ours, causes others to suffer pangs of conscience because of their sinful lives. In an attempt to make themselves look or feel better, they may spread evil rumors against you. The foolish woman retaliates by pointing out flaws in the other person, by trying to "get even." The wise woman looks beyond the moment to her ultimate reward in heaven. She recalls that she is in good company, that of Stephen, other Christian martyrs, the prophets, and of Christ, himself, who, when reviled, reviled not again. In this she rejoices.

CONCLUSION: The foolish woman sees no happiness in Christ, for she insists on her own way, her own rights. She is not willing to see her old self crucified with him. She continues to seek happiness in worldly pleasures, reveling in acts of a sinful nature, never satisfied with what she possesses; centering her life around things.

The wise woman finds true happiness in her relationship with God through Christ. She realizes her dependence on God; she mourns for her own sins and those of the world but finds comfort in a life cleansed by godly sorrow that leads to repentance; she submits her life to God's control; she continues to hunger and thirst for righteousness, finds fulfillment in Christ; because she is the recipient of God's mercy, her compassion leads her to forgive those who wrong her, to do good to them; her purity of heart gives her true insight so that she can see God; she rejoices in the peace that passes understanding; because she sees in being persecuted for righteousness' sake she is identified with Christ, in the company of saints, she rejoices as she looks forward to her reward in heaven.

DAILY BIBLE READINGS:
Sunday: Proverbs 3:13-15, happiness in wisdom
Monday: Hebrews 12:5-11, happiness in discipline
Tuesday: 1 Peter 5:5-10, happiness in suffering
Wednesday: Matthew 5:3-12, happiness upside down
Thursday: 2 Corinthians 7:8-12, sorrow into happiness
Friday: Luke 6:27-36, happiness in mercy
Saturday: Acts 5:12-42, rejoicing in persecution
MEMORY VERSES:
Philippians 1:9-11, approve what is excellent

Chapter 10

The Wise Woman Knows
PEACE

The foolish woman may seek peace at any price. She knows that eating a cookie just before dinner may cause her three year old to refuse to eat the nutritious food she has prepared for him. He cries when she refuses the treat. It is easier for her to give him the cookie than to endure his fretting or get him interested in helping her set the table or in a new game.

Her attitude may be, "Anything goes; don't rock the boat." Perhaps her husband is not a Christian and wants her to participate in an activity which would violate her conscience. Rather than explaining lovingly to him why the activity would be bad for her, perhaps for the children, she gives in and accompanies him.

The foolish woman enjoys the company of a group of women whose standards are not those her parents taught her. At one of their parties she is offered an alcoholic beverage. She says to herself, "I can't afford to offend these girls. One little drink won't hurt."

While the foolish woman is having coffee with friends, several of them make snide remarks about a friend or perhaps about the church. Although she knows the remarks are unkind, perhaps untrue, she refuses to take sides. She does not want to offend anyone, so she keeps quiet.

The wise woman accepts the peace Christ promised and assumes her own responsibility to achieve and maintain peace. She knows that true peace comes from being right, first, with God. She recognizes that her home will be a haven of peace when she has the courage to guide her children with compassion to paths that lead to their ultimate well being. Because she is submissive and considerate of her husband, he will be willing to listen to her explanation of her convictions in a meek and quiet spirit.

Peace is not only a state of quiet and tranquility, freedom from disturbance or agitation. It is also purpose, acceptance, repose, and trust.

The wise woman's purpose is to be a Christian wife who will complement her husband according to God's plan. If he is a Christian, she will do all in her power to help him reach his potential in service to God. If he is not a Christian, she will do her best to win him, not by words, but by her purity and reverence of life (1 Peter 3:1).

The single woman's purpose is to be "concerned about the Lord's affairs. Her aim is to be devoted to the Lord in both body and spirit" (1 Corinthians 7:34).

In patiently guiding her children in God's way, the Christian mother directs them in the paths of peace.

Faced with unpleasant circumstances she can not change, the wise woman accepts them and does her best to find repose in the Lord's promise to be with her. She will trust in "him who is able to do immeasurable more than all we ask or imagine, according to his power that is at work within us" (Ephesians 3:20 NIV).

I. There is NO REAL PEACE for the foolish. They may seek peace in various ways, but when trouble comes, they lack the inner peace that sustains a Christian. God was offended by the sinfulness of Israel, but he was always ready to forgive; over and over he sent his prophets to warn them:

> "Peace, peace, to those far and near," says the Lord. "And I will heal them."
> But the wicked are like the tossing sea, which cannot rest, whose waves cast up mire and mud.
> "There is no peace," says my God, "for the wicked."
> (Isaiah 57:19b-21 NIV).

A. The wicked are trapped by their own schemes, according to Bildad in his discourse with the suffering Job. Quite often today what the foolish thought would bring them prosperity and peace brings disgrace and destruction. The ancient speaker might well be describing a current event:

> Indeed, the light of the wicked goes out,
> And the flame of his fire gives no light.
> The light in his tent is darkened,
> And his lamp goes out above him.
> His vigorous stride is shortened,
> And his own scheme brings him down.
> For he is thrown into the net by his own feet,

And he steps on the webbing.
A snare seizes him by the heel,
And a trap snaps shut on him.
A noose for him is hid in the ground,
And a trap for pain is on the path.
All around terrors frighten him,
And harry him at every step.
His strength is famished,
And calamity is at his side.
His skin is devoured by disease,
The first-born of death devours his limbs.
He is torn from the security of his tent,
And they march him before the king of terrors. (Job 18:5-14 NASV)

B. The lot of the wicked is tribulation and distress. None who choose not to follow God's plan for his children will escape the trials they bring upon themselves. Having their own way leads them in the wrong way: "But for those who are self-seeking and who reject the truth and follow evil, there will be wrath and anger. There will be trouble and distress for every human being who does evil" (Romans 2:8,9a NIV).

II. PEACE REQUIRES EFFORT. The person who wants to live a peaceful life must pursue it through the proper attitudes and channels. It is not going to "drop as the gentle dews from heaven."

A. By following the principles taught by inspired writers, we can live at peace with others: Peter quotes from Psalms 34:12-16 as he outlines the wise course for Christians:

Finally, all of you, live in harmony with one another; be sympathetic, love as brothers, be compassionate and humble. Do not repay evil with evil or insult with insult, but with blessing, because to this end you were called so that you may inherit a blessing. For,
"Whoever would love life and see good days
must keep his tongue from evil and his lips from
deceitful speech.
He must turn from evil and do good;
he must seek peace and pursue it.
For the eyes of the Lord are on the righteous
and his ears are attentive to their prayers
but the face of the Lord is against
those who do evil" (1 Peter 3:8-12 NIV).

B. Christians are taught to do everything in their power to live peaceably with everyone. This includes being sure we are right, and even when we are right and the other person wrong, we are not to repay them in kind but to do good instead. This does not mean we will not have enemies. Jesus did. But we are to follow his example in doing good and praying for them. Remember, from the cross he prayed, "Father, forgive them, for they know not what they do."

In the Roman letter, Paul outlines the course we are to take in our pursuit of peace:

> Do not repay anyone evil for evil. Be careful to do what is right in the eyes of everybody. If it is possible, as far as it depends on you, live at peace with everyone. Do not take revenge, my friends, but leave room for God's wrath, for it is written: "It is mine to avenge; I will repay," says the Lord. On the contrary:
>
> > "If your enemy is hungry, feed him;
> > if he is thirsty, give him something to drink.
> > In doing this, you will heap burning coals on his head."
>
> Do not be overcome by evil, but overcome evil with good. (Romans 12:17-21 NIV).

C. One reason that Christians are to be interested in those who govern them and in the affairs of government is that they may be free to live a peaceful, devoted life. We who live in a free country find this relatively easy to do. Out temptation is to be apathetic, to be unconcerned about those who represent and govern us. But suppose you lived in a country where you might be arrested for owning a Bible or for gathering with others for worship in an "unauthorized" service? Perhaps you then might be more zealous in your prayers! Paul, in writing to Timothy, urged that "supplications, prayers, intercessions, and thanksgivings be made for all men, for kings and all who are in high positions, that we may lead a quiet and peaceable life, godly and respectful in every way" (1 Timothy 2:1,2 RSV).

D. We are to be especially considerate of fellow Christians, that we may live in peace and build each other up. When we must differ with them in matters of faith, it should be as mature Christians, with concern for their souls and ours. We are to love them earnestly, from the heart.

In matters of opinion, we certainly should be ready and willing to yield in the interest of peace. Paul devoted all the fourteenth chapter of Romans to a discussion of the proper attitude toward the weak and those who differ with us on matters of opinion. He points out very forcefully that it is the Lord who will judge the action of each, that we who may be stronger are to be very careful to do nothing that would cause the weak to stumble: "So do not let what is good to you be spoken of as evil. For the kingdom of God does not mean food and drink but righteousness and peace and joy in the Holy Spirit; he who thus serves Christ is acceptable to God and approved by men. Let us then pursue what makes for peace and for mutual upbuilding" (Romans 14:16-19 RSV).

We should always have a positive attitude toward our brothers and sisters in Christ, being always ready to build them up rather than tearing them down. We should do our best to understand the emotional and physical demands made on our ministers, elders, and deacons. We should support them enthusiastically and cooperate in every way possible. Just as we are attentive to the physical needs of the babes in our families, we must be concerned for the spiritual welfare of new Christians. Paul cites Christ's sacrifice for us as motivation for our regard for one another:

> For God has not destined us for wrath, but for obtaining salvation through our Lord Jesus Christ, who died for us, that we may live together with Him. Therefore encourage one another, and build up one another, just as you are doing. But we request of you, brethren, that you appreciate those who diligently labor among you, and have charge over you in the Lord and give you instruction, and that you esteem them highly in love because of their work. Live in peace with one another. And we urge you, brethren, admonish the unruly, encourage the fainthearted, help the weak, be patient with all men (1 Thessalonians 5:9-14 NASV).

E. The woman who lives in strife and upheaval is exhibiting earthly, sensual, devilish wisdom. The wise woman, by her good life, demonstrates the wisdom from above, pure and peaceable. The result of such a life is a harvest of righteousness: "But the wisdom that comes from heaven is first of all pure; then peace loving, considerate, submissive, full of mercy and good fruit, impartial and sincere. Peacemakers who sow in peace raise a harvest of righteousness" (James 3:17, 18 NIV).

III. GOD IS THE AUTHOR OF PEACE. We have just stressed our part in seeking and pursuing peace, but we must not forget that peace, like every blessing, comes from God. Paul refers frequently to him as "the God of peace" (1 Thessalonians 5:23, etc.). Someone has said we should pray as if everything depended on God and work as if everything depended on us. This is something of the same situation. Just as we are utterly helpless to secure our own salvation if it had not been for God's loving provision through Jesus Christ, yet we must do our part in accepting his gift according to his plan.

The psalmist, David, extolled the many blessings which come from God. In Psalms 29:11 he declares, "The Lord gives strength to his people; the Lord blesses his people with peace."

A. It is through Jesus Christ that the peace of God is made available to all mankind. It took a miracle to convince Peter of this fact, but he gladly then proclaimed it to the household of Cornelius:

> I now realize how true it is that God does not show favoritism but accepts men from every nation who fear him and do what is right. This is the message God sent to the people of Israel, telling the good news of peace through Jesus Christ, who is Lord of all (Acts 10:34-36 NIV).

1. While preparing his disciples to accept his departure from them, Jesus promised the coming of the Holy Spirit, the comforter, and that they would share in his peace, "Peace I leave with you; my peace I give you. I do not give to you as the world gives. Do not let your hearts be troubled and do not be afraid."

We think of peace as being free of stress and trouble. Jesus had demonstrated to his followers, time and again, the peace that comes in turbulent times to one who is in complete harmony with God. They had seen him walk on the water. He slept peacefully when the boat in which they were riding was tossed by a storm.

"Teacher, do you not care if we perish?" his anxious disciples cried as they awakened him.

"Peace! Be still!" he rebuked the wind, calming the sea.

"Why are you afraid? Have you no faith?" he said to the fearful ones, who were filled with awe at this exhibition of his own inner peace and power (Mark 4:35-41 RSV).

They saw further demonstrations of his divine calm as he approached the ordeal of the cross. He warned that they would scatter and leave him alone; he told them plainly the source of his strength when he then assured them, "Yet I am not alone, for the Father is with me. I have said this to you, that in me you may have peace. In the world you have tribulation; but be of good cheer, I have overcome the world" (John 16:32,33 RSV).

When confronted with a mob of soldiers and officers, after praying in the garden, knowing all that was to befall him, he asked calmly, "Whom do you seek?"

"Jesus of Nazareth," they answered.

"I am he," was the unwavering reply.

His majesty so overwhelmed them that they fell to the ground. He asked again whom they sought and assured them that he was the man. Impetuous Peter attempted to defend him and cut off Malcus' ear, which Jesus restored, saying "Put your sword into its sheath; shall I not drink the cup which the Father has given me?" (John 18:1-11).

He displayed the peace of purpose throughout the mockery of his trial before Annas and Pilate. When the latter, urged on by the cry of "Crucify him, crucify him!" from the mob led by the chief priests and officers demanded, "Where are you from?" Jesus gave no answer.

"You will not speak to me? Do you not know that I have power to release you, and power to crucify you?" the fearful Pilate shouted.

"You would have no power over me unless it had been given you from above," Jesus replied calmly (John 19:6,9-11).

As the anxious disciples trembled at the foot of the cross, they beheld his majestic peace as he prayed, "Father, forgive them; for they know not what they do;" and as he cried out at the end, "Father, into thy hands I commit my spirit" (Luke 23:34,46).

2. This peace has been left to us. May we, as wise women, remember that this assurance bequeathed by Christ is available to us. Look to his example when you need calm for troubled waters, peace during persecution, strength to overcome the world! "Let the peace of Christ rule in your hearts, to which indeed you were called in the one body. And be thankful. Let the word of Christ dwell in you richly...And whatever you do, in word or deed, do everything in the name of the Lord Jesus, giving thanks to God the Father through him" (Colossians 3:14-16a, 17 RSV).

B. WE MUST OBEY to obtain peace in Christ. Just as we noted above that tribulation and distress are promised the foolish, or wicked, peace is as binding a promise to those who do good. "For he will render to every man according to his works: to those who by patience in well-doing seek for glory and honor and immortality, he will give eternal life...glory and honor and peace for every one who does good" (Romans 1:7,10a RSV).

From the divine viewpoint, doing good is being obedient; we show our love and appreciation to Christ by being obedient.

Jesus said, "If you love me, you will obey my command" (John 14:15 NIV).

We must remind ourselves again and again that it is possible to think we are obeying Christ when we may be following traditions of men. No place is this made more clear than at the conclusion of the sermon on the mount.

"Not everyone who says to me, 'Lord, Lord,' will enter the kingdom of heaven, but only he who does the will of my Father who is in heaven.

Many will say to me on that day, 'Lord, Lord, did we not prophesy in your name, and in your name drive out demons and perform many miracles?'

Then I will tell them plainly, 'I never knew you. Away from me, you evildoers!' " (Matthew 7:21-23 NIV).

His commands for the person who is seeking his peace are, first, to become a part of his body, the church. Inspired writers have recorded his great commission in Acts 2:38; Matthew 28:19, 20; Mark 16:15,16; John 20:30,31. We learn from these that one must believe that Jesus is the Christ, the son of God. This faith is produced by reading or hearing the testimony of those who were with him as recorded in the four gospels. You must be willing to confess your faith in him and to turn from a life of sin--which is any life not purified by the blood of Christ. You then are ready to be buried with him in baptism, putting off your old self and arising a new person who can say with Paul, "I have been crucified with Christ and I no longer live, but Christ lives in me. The life I live in the body, I live by faith in the Son of God, who loved me and gave himself for me" (Galatians 2:20 NIV).

Having been baptized into Christ, you are ready to live an entirely new life in him. In his letter to the Romans, Paul makes this change very clear: "How could we live in sin a moment longer? Have you forgotten that all of us who were baptized into Jesus Christ were, by that very action, sharing in his death? We were dead and buried with him in baptism, so that just as he was raised from the dead by that splendid revelation of the Father's power so we too might rise to life on a new plane altogether. If we have, as it were, shared his death, let us rise and live our new lives in him!" (Romans 6:3-5 P).

IV. TO BE SPIRITUALLY MINDED IS PEACE. This new you will want to follow Christ every day, to walk in the spirit, not after the flesh. This is really living! It truly is a life full of new purpose, infinite trust in the Lord and in his ability to lead us in the new and living way, acceptance of our share of suffering with Christ, and repose effected by the knowledge that God and Christ are with us.

Paul points out that we have an entirely new perspective: "The carnal attitude sees no further than natural things. But the spiritual attitude reaches out after the things of the spirit. The former attitude means, bluntly, death: the latter means life and inward peace" (Romans 8:5,6 P). The same writer gives very explicit instructions on the things to be avoided by one who walks by the Spirit so that the fruits of the Spirit may be borne in the new life:

> So I say, live by the Spirit, and you will not gratify the desires of the sinful nature. For the sinful nature desires what is contrary to the Spirit, and the Spirit what is contrary to the sinful nature. They are in conflict with each other, so that you do not do what you want. But if you are led by the Spirit, you are not under law. The acts of the sinful nature are obvious: sexual immorality, impurity and debauchery; idolatry and witchcraft; hatred, discord, jealousy, fits of rage, selfish ambition, dissensions, factions and envy; drunkenness, orgies, and the like. I warn you, as I did before, that those who live like this will not inherit the kingdom of God. But the fruit of the Spirit is love, joy, peace, patience, kindness, goodness, faithfulness, gentleness, and self-control. Against such things there is no law. Those who belong to Christ Jesus have crucified the sinful nature with its passions and desires. Since we live by the Spirit, let us keep in step with the Spirit (Galatians 5:16-25 NIV).

This new, spiritual life produces "peace that passes understanding." Remember, the carnal mind can not understand the things of the Spirit. They are foolishness to the worldly-minded person. He simply can not understand the value of giving up worldly pleasures to devote one's self to Christ. He just does not comprehend that the Christian is the happiest person on earth while he looks forward to heavenly bliss forever and ever. This life in Christ overflows with joy.

> Rejoice in the Lord always; again I will say, Rejoice. Let all men know your forbearance. The Lord is at hand. Have no anxiety about anything, but in everything by prayer and supplication with thanksgiving let your requests be made known to God. And the peace of God, which passes all understanding,

will keep your hearts and your minds in Christ Jesus. (Philippians 4:4-7 RSV)

CONCLUSION: The foolish woman seeks peace at any price, or she may depend on others to give her peace, not realizing that she has a responsibility to live at peace with others. While seeking worldly peace, she may miss entirely the peace provided by God to those who love and obey him.

The wise woman assumes her responsibility to do her best to live at peace with all. She has committed her life to the Lord, casts her anxiety on him, and enjoys the peace that the world can not understand.

DAILY BIBLE READINGS:
Sunday: Job 18:5-14, wickedness in a trap
Monday: 1 Peter 3:8-17, pursuit of peace
Tuesday: Psalms 28, The Lord, our peace
Wednesday: Romans 14:1-23, disagreeing agreeably
Thursday: 1 Thessalonians 5:5-23, living in Christian peace
Friday: Luke 22:39-23:47, divine peace in trial
Saturday: Philippians 4:4-9, peace that the world can not understand
MEMORY VERSES: Philippians 4:4-9

Chapter 11

The Wise Woman Knows
CONTENTMENT

This study might well be considered an extension of the previous lesson. One who is at peace with herself and with God is content. But what are the ingredients of contentment? Why should it be one of our goals? How important an ingredient is contentment in our lives? Just what IS contentment, anyway?

Of course the dictionary defines contentment as "being content." It is interesting that, in defining content, the Latin word, from which our English word derives, *contentus*, literally means "to hold together, restrain." The definition then given by Webster is, "having desires limited to that which one has, satisfied."

Apparently, if we "have it all together" and practice restraint, we can be content. It includes the sense of well being which comes from many of the things we have already discussed in these lessons: knowing who we are, where we are going, how we are going to get there. These might apply to mundane goals, but the Christian adds the vital goals of knowing God, Jesus Christ, and the Holy Spirit through the scriptures and letting them guide us as we grow to spiritual maturity.

Much contentment comes from deciding what is important, what is not. Williams' encyclopedia quotes an old story which illustrates "having it all together" beautifully:

> A bishop who was contented and cheerful through a long period of trial, when asked the secret of his contentment, said: "I will tell you. I make a right use of my eyes."
> "Please explain."
> "Most willingly," was the answer.
> "First I look up to heaven and remember that my principal business is to get there. Then I look down upon the earth and think how small a place I shall occupy when I am buried. Then I look around and see the many who are in all respects much

worse off than I am. Then I learn where true happiness lies, where all our care ends, and how little reason I have to complain. (Leewin B. Williams, *Encyclopedia of Wit Humor and Wisdom*. No. 700, p. 101.)

I. WHEN SHOULD YOU NOT BE CONTENT? Yes, let's look at the negative before we delve into the positive. A bullfrog dozing on the river bank, a cow chewing her cud as she stands in the shade of a tree, languidly driving away pesky flies with her bushy tail, are content. The frog is not aware that he may be gulped down by a huge snake slithering near, nor the cow that she may be driven to slaughter tomorrow. To acheive true contentment, we must look inward, outward, and up.

A. You should not be content when you are not doing your best. Your child may be perfectly happy when he brings home a C or even an F on his report card. But neither you nor his teacher is content because you know that he is capable of doing better; if he is not, then you, too, should be content. Over and over we have stressed that each of us is endowed with individual talent, ability. Our abilities vary. We are responsible only for using what we have. But we must be careful to recognize our abilities and develop them. Then we must use them, for our own happiness, and to be pleasing to the Lord: "Serve one another with the particular gifts God has given each of you, as faithful dispensers of the magnificently varied grace of God," Peter urged (1 Peter 4:10 P).

God expects us to do our best. Again and again in sacred writing we read: "Giving all diligence," "Make every effort," "Do your utmost," "Try your hardest," are admonitions from various translations. They indicate that because God has made it possible for us to escape the corruption of the world and partake of his divine nature, we must put real effort into acquiring the Christian graces, enumerated by Peter in 2 Peter 1:3-11. Having outlined the components of spiritual growth, the writer again exhorts to action: "Give diligence to make your calling and election sure; be the more zealous to confirm your call and election; set your minds on endorsing by your conduct the fact that God has called and chosen you; exert yourselves to clinch God's choice and calling of you" (2 Peter 1:10 KJ, RSV, P, NEB).

Our teen-agers might say, "Get with it!"

We might add, expect the best of yourself; do not be content with less. But do not set unrealistic goals for yourself, not in keeping with your talents. Help each child to do her best, but do not expect one to be a rubber stamp of yourself, her father, or of an older sister or brother. She will be happiest when she competes with herself and knows she has done a good job.

B. You should not be content with an environment detrimental to your spiritual life or that of your children. You should not be satisfied to live on welfare if you are physically able and have the ability to do better. Our government has been for several years providing programs to help those who have not been able to cope in our society to recognize their abilities and train themselves to do better.

When God saw that not even ten righteous people could be found in wicked Sodom, he sent angels to take Lot and his family away before destroying that city and its sister in evil, Gomorrah (Genesis 18,19). Lot paid the price for having chosen the well-watered plain of the Jordan and "pitched his tents near Sodom" (Genesis 13). Because she disobeyed God's command not to look back, his wife became a pillar of salt. Today husbands may be pushed into evil companionship or physical exhaustion in jobs not suited to their abilities by demanding, unspiritual wives. Worldly ambition may cause a family to remain in an environment which may cause them to lose their souls. Paul cautions Christians against the love of money with its attendant temptations, "But you, man of God, flee from all this." Sometimes a move or retreat is our best strategy. Paul also advised young Timothy, "Flee the evil desires of youth, and pursue righteousness, faith, love and peace, *along with* those who call on the Lord out of a pure heart" (1 Timothy 6:11; 2 Timothy 2:22 NIV).

C. You must never be content in doing evil. Some might think that the brothers of Joseph had some cause for their jealousy because of Jacob's undisguised partiality to him. However, he was their brother, and at least Reuben and Levi had enough compassion to prevent their killing him. You will remember that the brothers had plotted his death, but Reuben suggested that he be cast into a pit, planning secretly to return Joseph to his father. Judah, seeing a band of Ishmaelites coming, suggested that Joseph be sold to them. The King James says, "And his brethren were content" (Genesis 37:27). The Bible does not tell us how the brothers felt during the long years when their father grieved for his son, but we do know that they were conscience stricken when Joseph finally revealed himself to them in Egypt after having risen to a position second only to the Pharoah. They could not face him comfortably: "And his brethren could not answer him; for they were troubled at his presence" (Genesis 45:3b KJ). We can be thankful that our loving God made provision, through Christ, for our forgiveness when we have been engulfed in sin--just as Joseph forgave his brethren and provided homes for them and his father in the most productive area in Egypt.

D. May you never be content with spiritual weakness in your life. Paul exhorted Timothy to "fight the good fight, holding on to faith and a good conscience. Some have rejected these and so have shipwrecked their faith" (1 Timothy 1:18c-19 NIV). The Hebrews were warned, "Take heed, brethren, lest there be in any of you an evil heart of unbelief, in departing from the living God" (Hebrews 3:12 KJ). As faith is obtained by hearing the word of God (Romans 10:17, it can be lost by neglect; but it can be strengthened by study of the word: "Desire the sincere milk of the word, that ye may grow thereby" (1 Peter 2:2b KJ).

II. THE WISE ARE CONTENT WITHOUT RICHES. Shakespeare wrote long ago:

> I swear tis better to be lowly born,
> And range with humble livers in content,
> Than to be perked up in a glistering grief,
> And wear a golden sorrow (Henry VIII, iii, 19).

As with many philosophies, this bit of wisdom had been proclaimed by inspired writers hundreds of years before they were penned by the master poet. Among the proverbs compiled by Solomon are the words of Agur the son of Jakeh, the oracle:

> Give me neither poverty nor riches;
> Feed me with the food that is my portion,
> Lest I be full and deny Thee and say,
>   "Who is the Lord?"
> Or lest I be in want and steal,
> And profane the name of my God. (Proverbs 30:8 NASV).

A. Paul warns very strongly against materialism. Once I thought, "Why? Why?" when I read in the newspapers of the arrest of a man who had been outstanding in the church; he was charged with fraud. It so happened that my daily reading that very day was 1 Timothy 6. I felt almost as if God had answered my question directly. He certainly, through Paul, had answered by his word:

> But if we have food and clothing, we will be content with that. People who want to get rich fall into temptation and a trap and

into many foolish and harmful desires that plunge men into ruin and destruction. For the love of money is a root of all kinds of evil. Some people, eager for money, have wandered from the faith and pierced themselves with many griefs (1 Timothy 6:8-10 NIV).

Are you tempted to say, "But, God, haven't you heard about inflation? How can we get along without a large savings account and big insurance policies? My husband and I both work; therefore we need two cars. And we certainly deserve some recreation. Surely it is not wrong for us to buy a boat and a camper or a house at the lake! And I'm too tired to cook after working all day; so we just have to eat out often. Have you noticed how the prices on the menu have gone up? Besides, with bread costing a dollar a loaf and hamburger meat more than $1.50 per pound, we can eat out about as economically as at home."

Note first that this scripture says *the love of money* leads to all kinds of evil. There are those who can acquire and use substantial wealth and remain true to the Lord, in fact, do much good with their money. There are those who have not been able to build fortunes who will lose their souls because of the wrong attitude toward money, making of it a false god. Later in this same chapter Paul commands that those who are rich must not be proud or trust in their riches. They are to do good, to be generous, and willing to share. "In this way they will lay up treasure for themselves as a firm foundation for the coming age, so that they may take hold of the life that is truly life," he concludes (1 Timothy 6:19 NIV).

B. The Bible teaches that the laborer is worthy of his hire, but it also teaches that laborers are not to be unreasonable in demands for higher wages. Many of the strikes, much of the unrest in the labor market today stem from demands for more and more money, more and more benefits. Of course the ideal situation between employer and employee is pictured in Ephesians 6:5-9, where slaves are told to render service as to the Lord, and masters are reminded to do the same thing, "knowing that both their Master and yours is in heaven."

John the Baptist told soldiers who heard him preach and wanted to know what they should do, "Rob no one by violence or by false accusation, and be content with your wages" (Luke 3:14 RSV).

Aid from various financial institutions is available to those who need help in being content with their wages. Some have said that money management is an art, but it can be learned. One woman can take her husband's salary, and by careful planning provide more satisfactory living than another can who goes to work and makes as much or more than her husband does. The former may help her husband to maintain a growing savings account while the latter may be always behind with the bills. One reason for this is a focus on things. Having things we want is not, in itself wrong. But when the quest for things brings discontent into our lives, we are treading on dangerous ground.

C. We must avoid covetousness, which is defined as greed, avarice, grasping. It can be a love for money or things so intense that it is called idolatry in one instance. Frequently it leads one to have an unhealthy desire for that which belongs to others. This, in turn, often leads to unlawful means of acquiring that which is coveted. A covetous person certainly is not content with what he has.

When asked to arbitrate in two brothers' dispute over their inheritance, Jesus warned, "Take heed, and beware of all covetousness; for a man's life does not consist in the abundance of his possiessions" (Luke 12:15 RSV). And in Hebrews we are told: "Keep your life free from love of money (covetousness, KJ), and be content with what you have; for he has said, 'I will never fail you nor forsake you.' Hence we can confidently say, 'The Lord is my helper, I will not be afraid; what can man do to me?' " (Hebrews 13:5,6 RSV).

III. CONTENTMENT IS NOT DEPENDENT ON CIRCUMSTANCES. Just as happiness is not determined by circumstances, neither is the ability to be content. In the same family, with identical environment, you may find one child disgruntled because she does not have what her friends have; her sister may be perfectly happy and content, thankful for what she does have. Paul had been born to favorable circumstances in a Jewis family, gave up his advantage to preach Christ. He suffered shipwreck, beatings, persecution from his own brethren. Yet he was able to write, while a prisoner in Rome,

> Not that I am alluding to want, for I have learned to find resources in myself whatever my circumstances. (Most translations say, "in whatever state I am, to be content.) I know what it is to be brought low, and I know what it is to have plenty. I have been very thoroughly initiated into the human lot with all its ups and downs--fullness and hunger,

plenty and want. I have strength for anything through him who gives me power. (I can do all things through Christ which strengtheneth me. KJ) (Philippians 4:11-13 NEB; parentheses added).

I chose the quotation from the New English Bible because of the phrase, "to find resources in myself." At first glance, we might think this is extreme self-dependence--"I am the master of my fate!" It stems, rather, from his complete identity with Christ: "It is not I, Christ liveth in me." He recognized the source of his strength. This permitted him to rise completely above his prison state and say, "Rejoice in the Lord always; again I will say, Rejoice...I rejoice in the Lord greatly..." (Philippians 4:4,10 RSV).

You have access to that same strength. You can be content whatever your circumstances. This does not mean it is wrong for us to try to improve unfavorable physical or spiritual circumstances. We are taught we should care for our own. We are not to be anxious about it, though. We have noted the Lord's promise never to forsake or fail us. Through his strength we can live happily and confidently.

Do you have the inner resources to be content with *yourself*? Are you tempted to say, "Oh, if I were So-and-So, I could do so much more for the Lord, or I could be so much happier?" A favorite childrens' story tells of a little girl who wished she were Susie because Susie had a long dress and a big doll. When her mother asked if Susie had a pretty white cat, a lovely red dress with a satin bow, and a brother, little Janie decided she really didn't want to be Susie after all. I'm sure you've heard the story that people were asked to place their burdens in a pile then select one they preferred. Each, after looking them all over, chose his own! Not only should we do our best to be happy with our circumstance--where we are--but also with what we are. Here again it is a matter of assessing our abilites and resources and using them to the best advantage. A little poem, whose author I do not know, expresses very clearly the importance of being one's self; it is entitled *How to be Happy*:

> De sunflower ain't no daisy
> An'de melon ain't no rose;
> Why is dey all so crazy to be
> Sumfin' else dat grows?
> Jes' stick to de place your planted
> An' do de bes' yo knows;
> De sunflower or de daisy--

De melon or de rose.
Don't be what yo' aint--
Jes' be what yo' is--
If yo' am not what you' are
Den yo' is not what yo' is.
If yo' is es' a lil' tadpole
Don't try to be a frog;
If yo' is de tail,
Don't try to be de dawg.
Pass de plate if yo' can't
Exhawt an' preach;
If yo' is es' a lil' pebble,
Don't try to be de beach;
When a man is what he isn't
Den he isn't what he is;
An as sure as I'se a-talkin'
He's a-gwine to get his.
(Used by permission; from *Encyclopedia of Wit, Humor, and Wisdom,* Williams, p. 101)

IV. GODLINESS WITH CONTENTMENT IS GREAT GAIN. Being merely content, as we have indicated before, is not sufficient. The most immoral person in town may be perfectly content; she may not have had the opportunity to know and do better, or she may have had the opportunity but spurned it. With the proliferation of religious error available on radio and TV, it is easy for a person to be so confused that she decides simply to have nothing to do with religion. This would be less tragic if the truth were not so readily available to most people in the world--certainly to everyone in the United States. Bibles can be bought at any dime store and will be furnished without charge by many churches. Study guides also are offered free of charge. You can know the *godliness* that produces *contentment.*

This godliness is not merely moral acts; many who embrace no form of religion live by a moral code that produces a high standard of living yet does not make them right with God. Neither is it merely refraining from evil. James M. Tolle defines godliness as "that reverence or respect for God which is the sincere feeling of the heart in view of His nature and character...Perhaps a better word for godliness would be *god-ward-ness,* a state of mind which accepts God as the sole object of its adoration and reverential respect, the central object of its trust, and the infallible source of all religious responsibility" (Tolle, *The Christian Graces*, p. 51).

A strong warning is given by Paul against teachers who commercialize religion. He gives equally strong admonition for the Christian to shun error and find reward in godliness:

> If anyone teaches false doctrines and does not agree to the sound instruction of our Lord Jesus Christ and to godly teaching, he is conceited and understands nothing. He has an unhealthy interest in controversies and arguments that result in envy, quarreling, malicious talk, evil suspicions and constant friction between men of corrupt mind, who have been robbed of the truth and who think that godliness is a means to financial gain.
>
> But godliness with contentment is great gain. . .But you, man of God, flee from all this and pursue righteousness, godliness, faith, love, endurance, and gentleness. Fight the good fight of faith. (1 Timothy 6:3-6; 11-12a NIV).

CONCLUSION: The wise woman recognizes that inner peace is not dependent on circumstance but on a right relationship with God stemming from her reverence for him and her trust in him which leads her into an obedient life, characterized by righteousness, godliness, faith, love, endurance, and gentleness. She is content.

The foolish woman seeks contentment in the ways of the world. She misses the way of godliness because she listens to teachers of false doctrine. Her love of money may lead her into thievery, extortion...all kinds of evil. She seeks external gratification and misses inner peace, contentment.

DAILY BIBLE READINGS:
Sunday: 2 Peter 1:3-11--Be content only with your best.
Monday: Genesis 13, 18, 19--Flee bad environment.
Tuesday: 1 Timothy 6:3-18--Be content with what you have.
Wednesday: 2 Timothy 2:15-24--Avoid contention; be content.
Thursday: Ephesians 6:5-9--Mutual respect produces contentment.
Friday: Luke 12:13-21--Beware of covetousness.
Saturday: Luke 12:22-34--Be anxious for nothing.
MEMORY VERSES:
Proverbs 30:8; 1 Timothy 6:8-10

Chapter 12

The Wise Woman Knows
HER WAY

With roads being changed and improved constantly, it is a wise traveler who takes direction from his travel bureau or obtains the latest map and follows it carefully. He would be foolish to take the direction of one who had traveled his projected road twenty years ago and offered to draw a map for him.

The traveler from earth to heaven, however, has no such problem, for the way was mapped by Jesus Christ and recorded by his faithful followers. She will need to be wary of maps that purport to be a new way, and she certainly will need to avoid byways.

Having determined that her goal is heaven, she will study the map (Bible) carefully, and as she travels, she will heed the inspired directions. She must be sure she is on the right road by making a proper entrance then follow the well marked road. She need not stumble in darkness, for the highway is well lighted.

She can travel confidently, enjoying the fellowship of pleasant companions along the way.

I. WATCH OUT FOR BYWAYS AND DETOURS! How foolish is the woman who depends on her instincts, even her conscience (if not educated properly), for direction. Have you ever had your directions confused--been turned around? I remember visiting at my sister's home where, to me, the sun rose in the north every single day. How patiently they explained to me that I was the one confused, that Good Old Sol continued to make his morning debut in the east. But it still *seemed* to me that he peeped over my horizon in the north. My instincts simply were not guiding me aright!

We dare not be satisfied with a way just because it seems right, for "There is a way that seems right to a man, but in the end it leads to death" (Proverbs 14:12 NIV).

A. The foolish person believes her course of action is right, that is, in her own eyes. She will not listen to counsel from those who have her interest at heart. The wise woman listens and changes course if necessary.

"The way of a fool is right in his own eyes, but a wise man listens to advice," is just as true today as it was when written many years ago (Proverbs 12:15 RSV).

One does have to be careful to heed the advice of the wise, for foolish advice can lead to destruction: "My son, if sinners entice you, do not consent. If they say, 'Come with us, let us lie in wait for blood, let us wantonly ambush the innocent! ...My son, do not walk in the way with them, hold back your foot from their paths; for their feet run to evil, and they make haste to shed blood...Such are the ways of all who get gain by violence; it takes away the life of its possessors'' (Proverbs 1:10,11,15-16,19 RSV).

A course of action may even appear to be all right from a human standpoint, but we must remember that, in our journey heavenward, we have to please our Lord, not the world. He has taught repeatedly that it is the inner man, not externals, that determine our standing in his sight:

"Every way of a man is right in his own eyes, but the Lord weighs the heart," (Proverbs 21:2 RSV).

B. Don't just follow the crowd. "Everyone's doing it; everyone's going," is the plaintive plea heard so often by parents of young people who are being subjected to peer pressure. They want to conform even if it means going contrary to values their parents have taught them. It is hard for them to understand that some ways that seem right are actually wrong. The majority is not always right. Jesus taught this convincingly as he warned: "Enter through the narrow gate. For wide is the gate and broad the road that leads to destruction, and many enter through it. But small is the gate and narrow the road that leads to life, and only a few find it" (Matthew 7:13,14 NIV).

C. You will have a hard time on the byways, the sinner's way. Young or old who violate principles of right will find it is true that "the way of the transgressor is hard" (Proverbs 13:15). Some may protest that it is easier to go with the crowd. In a way that may be true, for we know it is easier to drift with the tide than to swim up stream. But we may miss our goal completely if we just drift along, not caring where we are headed, failing to put forth the effort to get where we want to go.

When you became a Christian, you surely intended to remain faithful. Maybe others in your family did not share your spiritual values, and it became easier to go partying on Saturday night and sleep late on Sunday morning. You missed one worship service or Bible study period, then another and another. As you fed less and less on God's word, you became weaker spiritually; it was harder for you to resist the temptation to put a pleasure trip or a golf game before your obligation to assemble with the saints for spiritual renewal.

In neglecting your immediate goal of regular Bible study and worship, you lost sight of your ultimate goal: remaining faithful to the Lord, walking with fellow Christians on the journey to eternity.

We always would do well to follow Paul's instruction to the Colossians:

> So then, just as you received Christ Jesus as Lord, continue to live in him, rooted and built up in him, strengthened in the faith as you were taught, and overflowing with thankfulness. See to it that no one takes you captive through hollow and deceptive philosophy, which depends on human tradition and the basic principles of this world rather than on Christ (Colossians 2:6-8 NIV).

To live in Christ is to follow his teachings, to gain spiritual strength through regular worship and Bible study. Thus we will avoid the danger of being led down a dark byway or a glittering side road that will lead only to destruction. Some of those byways are false religions, where the teachers actually do not believe in the virgin birth of Christ--or they may not be following Christ at all but teaching Buddhism or the worship of some other false god. Some times the path that is nearest the right road may prove more tempting than that which is blatantly wrong. At all times you must be on guard against false teaching in the name of Christ. The air waves, both on radio and television, are full of it; persuasive speakers make their false teachings sound so logical. You can and must know for your self the teaching of the New Testament so that you can recognize that which is false.

Paul warned repeatedly of the danger of false teachers, and he was echoing the same teaching by Jesus Christ. In his farewell visit with the Ephesian elders, Paul warned: "I know that after I leave savage wolves will come in among you and will not spare the flock. Even from your own number men will arise and distort the truth in order to draw away disciples after them. So be on your guard!" (Acts 20:29-31a NIV). Remember, Jesus told those who claimed to have done wonderful things in his name while disobeying God, "Depart from me, you evildoers" (Matthew 7:23 RSV).

II. STUDY THE ROAD MAP. THE ROAD IS WELL MARKED. The New Testament is our road map today. It is clear and understandable, but if you need help, be sure to follow one who is following the map faithfully. If you are seeking the truth, with a good and honest heart, you will find it. David was referred to as a man after God's own heart, this despite the sinful acts he committed. He acknowledged freely his sins and, with a penitent heart, sought forgiveness. He praised the Lord continually. We can well emulate his idea:

> Search me, O God, and know my heart;
> Try me and know my anxious thoughts;
> And see if there be any hurtful way in me,
> And lead me in the everlasting way (Psalms 139:23,24 NASV).

Like David, we must be willing to let the Lord lead us in the right way. We must have confidence in him as our guide to a happy journey through life. We can join the psalmist in saying, "You have made known to me the path of life; you will fill me with joy in your presence, with eternal pleasures at your right hand" (Psalms 16:11 NIV).

A. Wisdom leads the prudent woman in the right way. Those who will heed instruction from the right source are not likely to be led into hurtful side roads. Wisdom is personified in parts of Proverbs; she has built her house and calls out, "Forsake your folly and live, and proceed in the way of understanding" (Proverbs 9:6 NASV).

B. On the path of wisdom, you can even run and will not stumble:

> Listen, my son, accept what I say,
>   and the years of your life will be many.
> I guide you in the way of wisdom
>   and lead you along straight paths.
> When you walk, your steps will not be hampered;
>   when you run, you will not stumble.
> Hold onto instruction, do not let it go;
>   guard it well, for it is your life.
> Do not set foot on the path of the wicked
>   or walk in the way of evil men.
> Avoid it, do not travel on it;
>   turn from it and go on your way (Proverbs 4:10-15 NIV).

Now you may ask, "Where is this way of wisdom?"

III. CHRIST IS THE WAY! When you are in Christ, you are on the express way. But even on such a well-marked way you still may be tempted to take a wrong turn; so you still must be guided by the word of God--your road map--and follow the signs, the commands and examples it supplies. Thus your way will be well lighted: When Jesus spoke again to the people, he said, "I am the light of the world. Whoever follows me will never walk in darkness, but will have the light of life" (John 8:12 NIV).

A. That Jesus would be a guide in the living way was foretold in Zechariah's inspired prophecy at the birth of John the Baptist:

> And you, my child, will be called a prophet of the Most High;
> for you will go on before the Lord to prepare the way for him,
> to give his people the knowledge of salvation
> through the forgiveness of their sins,
> because of the tender mercy of our God, by which the rising sun
> will come to us from heaven
> to shine on those living in darkness and in the shadow of death,
> to guide our feet in the path of peace (Luke 1:76-79 NIV).

John's mission was to be a forerunner for Christ, to prepare the way for the Christ, the Messiah who had been so long expected by the Israelites.

B. Jesus is THE way. Toward the end of his ministry, Jesus was preparing his apostles for separation from him. They had walked so closely with him that it was hard for them to think of his leaving them. Peter demanded that he be allowed to go with Jesus, declaring that he would lay down his life for his Lord. Reassuring them, Jesus declared that he was going to prepare a place for them, in his Father's house where there are many mansions, or rooms.

"You know the way to the place where I am going," he concluded.

Thomas said to him, "Lord, we don't know where you are going, so how can we know the way?"

Jesus answered, "I am the way and the truth and the life. No one comes to the Father except through me" (John 14:4-6 NIV).

C. What better road sign could we ask? It is not as if there were an alternate route. Many times when we are planning a trip, we can choose the better of several ways. But there is only ONE way to the Father, that is through his son, Jesus Christ. The wise woman will hasten to enter the way, if she is not already on this road to heaven. Paul has told us plainly how we get into Christ; we are baptized into him. (Romans 6:3,4; Galatians 3:26,27). The foolish woman may contend that she was saved the moment she believed, or she may recount an experience which convinced her she is saved, that baptism is not necessary. After saying that one who does not enter the sheepfold by the door but climbs in by another is a thief and robber, Jesus concluded, "I am the door, if anyone enters by me, he will be saved" (John 10:1,9 RSV).

D. Having entered the way, the wise woman travels happily in this new, living way. Many passages describe the Christian life, but few make it more plain than Colossians 1:9-14:

> We have not ceased to pray for you and to ask that you may be filled with the knowledge of His will in all spiritual wisdom and understanding, so that you may walk in a manner worthy of the Lord, to please Him in all respects, bearing fruit in every good work and increasing in the knowledge of God; strengthened with all power, according to His glorious might, for the attaining of all steadfastness and patience; joyously giving thanks to the Father, who has qualified us to share in the inheritance of the saints in light. For He delivered us from the domain of darkness, and transferred us to the kingdom of His beloved Son, in whom we have redemption, the forgiveness of sins (NASV).

Take your pencil and paper. Read the above passage thoughtfully and list phrases describing the new life. I found at least twelve. Can you find more? You might go back up to verse four of the same chapter and note Paul's commendation of the Colossians' faith in Christ Jesus and their love for all the saints.

Continuing our comparison of the Christian life to expressway travel, we look at another passage where we see that the "toll" was paid by the blood of Jesus. He might be considered the patrolman, for he acts as our high priest. Good road signs along the way give us assurance; we are not undecided as we travel. Pleasant traveling companions are considerate of us and stimulate us to love and good deeds:

> Since therefore, brethren, we have confidence to enter the holy place by the blood of Jesus, by a new and living way which He inaugurated for us through the veil, that is, His flesh, and since we have a great priest over the house of God, let us draw near with a sincere heart in full assurance of faith, having our hearts sprinkled clean from an evil conscience and our bodies

washed with pure water. Let us hold fast the confession of our hope without wavering, for He who promised is faithful; and let us consider how to stimulate one another to love and good deeds, not forsaking our own assembling together, as is the habit of some, but encouraging one another; and all the more, as you see the day drawing near (Hebrews 10:19-25 NASV).

We might even consider our assembling to worship rest stops along the way. We should leave those meetings refreshed spiritually, ready for service and good works.

IV. STAY ON THE "KING'S HIGHWAY!" Though we are guided with power from above and have the encouragement of others, we still must be alert as we travel to eternity. Satan never gives up and his agents may beckon you to dangerous byways. There are warning signs along the way: "The highway of the upright avoids evil; he who guards his way guards his soul" (Proverbs 16:17 NIV).

A. God's word guides the traveler and lights his way. Just as your faith initially was produced by hearing God's word (Romans 10:17), you must depend on the word to guide you each day. Remember, the Bereans were called more noble than others because they searched the scriptures daily to see if the things they were being told were true (Acts 17:11).

The wise woman has marked her road map to heaven and keeps her eye on the road! God's word lights the way for her: "Thy word is a lamp unto my feet, and a light unto my path" (Psalms 119:105 KJ).

B. Unlike the road maps for our earthly travel, our heavenly guide never changes. We have tried using maps from the 1960's as we drove from Texas to California. We missed some of the interstate highways which simply were not there when the maps were printed. Although we may gain interest and insight from translations which keep pace with our changing language, God's word, itself, never changes; it will never pass away. Jesus said, "Heaven and earth will pass away, but My words will not pass away" (Luke 21:33 NASV).

If we get on the wrong road, it will not be because the map has changed; it will be simply because we failed to know and follow our guide: "Ye do err, not knowing the Scriptures nor the power of God," Jesus said. (Matthew 22:29 KJ).

C. The wise woman finds that she's really living as she travels the royal road. There are those who want to "sow their wild oats, to live it up" before becoming Christians. Do you suppose complaining, long-faced "Christians" have left the impression with them that God's way is not a good way? Paul said widows who plunged into worldly pleasure were dead while they lived (1 Timothy 5:6). Those who remain in sin are the foolish ones, missing out on life that is full and rewarding: "In the way of righteousness is life, and in its pathway there is no death" (Proverbs 12:28 NASV).

While presenting himself as the door to the sheepfold, then as the good shepherd, Jesus said, "I came that they may have life, and have it abundantly" (John 10:10 RSV).

D. At the end of the road, the wise woman will claim her reservation. Waiting for her there will be the Lord Jesus and many of her loved ones who have gone on before. She will live eternally in the presence of God and his angels, with Abraham, Isaac, and Jacob...and the apostles in the mansions Jesus assured them he had gone to prepare. Her reward will come because she freed herself from sin to become a slave to God:

> But now having been freed from sin and enslaved to God, you derive your benefit, resulting in sanctification, and the outcome, eternal life. For the wages of sin is death, but the free gift of God is eternal life in Christ Jesus our Lord (Romans 6:22, 23 NASV).

CONCLUSION: The wise woman studies God's word, the map from earth to heaven. Confidently, she enters "The Way," and avoids byways as she travels with the saints to mansions prepared for them.

While insisting on her own way, the foolish woman misses THE WAY to eternal life with God.

DAILY BIBLE READINGS:
Sunday: Colossians 2:6-8, Shun the byways.
Monday: Proverbs 4:10-15, the way of wisdom
Tuesday: Luke 1:66-79, forerunner to the path of peace
Wednesday: John 13:33-14:7, The Way
Thursday: John 10:1-13, The Door to the sheepfold
Friday: Colossians 1:3-14, the right way
Saturday: Hebrews 10:19-25, the new and living way
MEMORY VERSES:
Proverbs 21:2; Matthew 7:13,14

Chapter 13

The Wise Woman Knows
HER DESTINATION

"Thoughts lead on to purpose; purposes go forth in action; actions form habits; habits decide character; and character fixes our destiny." These lines written by Tyron Edwards are appropriate to this concluding lesson in our series of studies on the importance of our knowing who we are, where we are going, and how to get there. Of course all Edwards' statement can be found in scripture, "For as he thinketh in his heart, so is he" (Proverbs 23:7a KJ).

The foolish woman has her thoughts fixed on worldly things, such as a husband just a bit more handsome than her neighbor's; a house somewhat more luxurious, a better car, finer clothes, more exciting trips and entertainment. The danger in this focus on things is that they do not satisfy. One thus motivated wants more and more. We become like the man who really was not land-greedy, in his own opinion; he just wanted to own all the land touching his! The wordly mind is fixed on the here and now and loses sight of the hereafter.

The wise woman has her affection set on things above. This does not mean, however, that she has an "expressway complex"--stopping only for emergencies, looking only toward her destination and missing all the beautiful sights, experiences, and associations along the way. Rather, her assurance of eternal salvation frees her from distractons along the way. Christ centered thoughts prompt her to follow his example in living, loving, serving, and devotion to God, the Father.

I. THE WISE WOMAN KEEPS HER ETERNAL GOAL IN MIND. Because she has chosen to give up worldly pleasures and become a partaker of the divine nature, her purpose is to "become mature, attaining to the whole measure of the fullness of Christ" (Ephesians 4:13 NIV). Her heart and mind are focused on heavenly things:

Since, then, you have been raised with Christ, set your hearts on things above, where Christ is seated at the right hand of God. Set your minds on things above, not on earthly things. For you died, and your life is now hidden with Christ in God. When Christ, who is your life, appears, then you also will appear with him in glory (Colossians 1:1-4 NIV)

A. Being "raised with Christ," she is living on a higher plane. But just how did this take place? Having heard the gospel, believed that Jesus is the son of God, determined to turn from a life of sin, she was ready to be buried with him in baptism. She was raised to a new life: "And you were buried with him in baptism, in which you were also raised with him through faith in the working of God, who raised him from the dead. And you, who were dead in trespasses and the uncircumcision of your flesh, God made alive together with him, having forgiven us all our trespasses" (Colossians 2:13,14 RSV).

B. Set your hearts on things above. You remember the intensity of desire you felt when you "set your heart" on a new toy, a lovely dress, going to college, getting that first date with the man of your dreams. Do you really feel that same yearning for heavenly things? Our will is involved here. The King James, in Colossians 3:2 says, "Set your affection on things above." You and I know that we really do not "fall in love." Because of association under favorable circumstances, we grew, or learned, to love the man who possessed qualities that attracted us. The Revised Standard says "Seek the things that are above," and Phillips says, "Reach out for the highest gifts of Heaven." Our spiritual desire grows as we feed on God's word, receive the encouragement of others in worship, find satisfaction in serving God by serving others. We must seek, or reach out for, these experiences which will point our thoughts and hearts above.

That's where Christ is, seated at the right hand of God. I really had very little interest in Tulsa, Oklahoma, until my daughter and her husband chose to make it their home. Because of my love for them, I soon developed an interest in their city with its lovely rose garden, museums, and many other opportunities for a good life. I am intensely interested in heaven because my savior is waiting there to welcome me to the mansions he has gone to prepare for those who love and obey him.

C. Set your minds on things above. Your mind will be set on what you put into it. Be honest with yourself. Do you spend more time reading the newspaper or watching television than you do in reading your Bible? Do you spend more time reading secular books and magazines than you do in reading literature written by Christians for the purpose of promoting your spiritual growth and that of the church? Do you examine the religious literature you read to be sure it is in accordance with God's word? I hesitate even to mention pornographic literature! Surely those of us who are trying to set our affections on things above do not allow Satan to tempt us to lust by feeding on such garbage. It is a sad commentary on our moral **climate that parents have to be very cautious in selecting motion pictures and television shows their children may watch.** Youngsters may argue, "Oh, Mother, I don't pay any attention to the bedroom scenes and the foul language. I just enjoy a good story."

I heard that one mother, being given that line, was in the process of preparing a salad for dinner. She calmly picked up a handful of peelings and cores and stirred them into the salad. The daughter was horrified.

"Mother!" she screamed. "You're ruining the salad!"

"I thought if you didn't mind filling your mind with garbage, you couldn't object to a little in your salad," was the wise reply.

The contrast between the sinful nature and that of the Spirit is drawn convincingly in the scriptures:

> Those who live according to the sinful nature have their minds set on what that nature desires; but those who live in accordance with the Spirit have their minds set on what the Spirit desires; The mind of sinful man is death, but the mind controlled by the Spirit is life and peace, because the sinful mind is hostile to God. It does not submit to God's law, nor can it do so. Those controlled by the sinful nature cannot please God...Therefore, brothers, we have an obligation--but it is not to the sinful nature, to live according to it. For if you live according to the sinful nature, you will die; but if by the Spirit you put to death the misdeeds of the body you will live, because those who are led by the Spirit of God are sons of God (Romans 8:5-8, 12-14 NIV).

We have a choice. We can live by walking by the Spirit; we can choose death if we persist in living according to the sinful nature. Paul pleads with us to walk by the Spirit, not to gratify the desires of the flesh, noting that the two ways of life are in constant conflict.

Now the deeds of the flesh are evident, which are: immorality, impurity, sensuality, idolatry, sorcery, enmities, strife, jealousy, outbursts of anger, disputes, dissensions, factions, envyings, drunkenness, carousings, and things like these, of which I forewarn you just as I have forewarned you that those who practive such things shall not inherit the kingdom of God. But the fruit of the Spirit is love, joy, peace, patience, kindness, goodness, faithfulness, gentleness, self-control; against such things there is no law. Now those who belong to Christ Jesus have crucified the flesh with its passions and desires (Galatians 5:19-24 NASV).

If your mind is set on the things of the flesh, then works of the flesh will follow; they will become habits hard to break. Your character will have degenerated--you will be dead in sin. But if your mind is set on things above, the fruits of the Spirit will be manifest in your life. Your character will attract others to share your spiritual destiny.

D. Your life is hidden with Christ in God. This is just another way of saying what Paul said after listing the works of the flesh and of the Spirit; Christians simply consider their old sinful nature crucified with Christ. As Paul said, "It is no longer I who live, but Christ who lives in me, and the life I now live in the flesh I live by faith in the Son of God, who loved me and gave himself for me" (Galatians 2:20 RSV).

What a comforting thought it is that our lives are actually hidden in Christ. God makes no record of sins committed by those who are "walking in the light," that is, living a righteous life, in Christ, to the best of their ability. We are told in 1 John 1:7 that those who thus walk are being cleansed from all sin by the blood of Christ. It would be a terrifying thought that one day we must stand before the judgment seat of God if we did not have as our mediator one who has lived on the earth and been tempted as we are tempted. Almost as a child gains courage by holding onto her mother's skirt while making an explanation to her father, we can come confidently before God's throne with our lives shielded in Christ. There we are assured of mercy and grace to help in our need--both now and at the end of the world (Hebrews 4:15,16).

II. CHRIST IS OUR LIFE. While on earth, Jesus said that he had come that we might have life and have it more abundantly (John 10:10). This abundance extends to all phases of our lives. Paul said, "And my God will meet all your needs according to his glorious riches in Christ Jesus" (Philippians 1:19 NIV). Although this does not assure us of every *want*, we can be sure that the necessities of life will be ours if we put the kingdom of God and his righteousness first. Jesus promised this in the sermon on the mount (Matthew 6:25-34).

We have at our disposal unlimited power according to Paul's prayer for the Ephesians: "Now to him who is able to do immeasurably more than all we ask or imagine, according to his power that is at work within us, to him be glory in the church and in Christ Jesus throughout all generations, for ever and ever!" (Ephesians 3:20 NIV).

God's bounty can overflow, through us, to others. It is up to us; if we sow sparingly, we can expect to reap sparingly. If we sow bountifully, we can also expect to reap bountifully. Someone has said we just need to "let go and let God." I wonder at times if we truly trust God and his promises through the scriptures. Do we really believe that Jesus wants to give us an abundant life? Paul wrote that God loves a cheerful giver and concluded, "And God is able to provide you with every blessing in abundance, so that you may always have enough of everything and may provide in abundance for every good work" (2 Corinthians 9:8 RSV).

Obviously, these promises are to those in Christ, those to whom Christ IS life. The foolish woman may go through a form of religion and expect to receive the promises while she has her heart set on worldly things. God knows our hearts and will deal with us accordingly. Paul warned the young preacher, Timothy:

> But realize this, that in the last days difficult times will come. For men will be lovers of self, lovers of money, boastful, arrogant, revilers, disobedient to parents, ungrateful, unholy, unloving, irreconcilable, malicious gossips, without self-control, brutal, haters of good, treacherous, reckless, conceited, lovers of pleasure rather than lovers of God; holding to **a form of godliness, although they have denied its power** (2 Timothy 3:1-5 NASV).

In sharp contrast to this is the wise woman whose life is bearing the fruit of the Spirit because Christ IS her life. Her love for God is manifest in her love for fellow Christians; her love for God is proved by her obedience to his commands (1 John 5:1-5). She is aware that in Christ she is traveling toward a glorious destiny: "And this is the testimony: God has given us eternal life, and this life is in his Son.

He who has the Son has life; he who does not have the Son of God does not have life" (1 John 5:11,12 NIV).

III. WE HAVE ETERNAL LIFE IN PROMISE. From the above passage we are not to assume that one who believes on the Son has eternal life unconditionally. But we are not to doubt that one so believing is promised eternal life; we have God's own testimony to that fact. The key is in verse 12: "He who has the Son has life; he who does not have the Son of God does not have life." One may *have* a fortune and *lose* it. One may *have* eternal life in promise and by his unfaithfulness *lose* the promised glory. In Revelations 2:10 we read, "Be thou faithful unto death, and I will give thee a crown of life." It is necessary for us to abide in the Son in order to receive the promise: "As for you, let that abide in you which you heard from the beginnings. If what you heard from the beginning abides in you, you also will abide in the Son and in the Father. And this is the promise which He Himself made to us: eternal life" (1 John 2:24, 25 NASV).

A. Through faith, the wise woman KNOWS her destination. This does not mean, however, that she should assume the attitude, "I have it made. I can just sit back and take it easy." Just as an athlete who has made the team must continue to train, a Christian must be as concerned about her spiritual welfare. Our attitude should be like that of the Apostle Paul:

> Not that I have already obtained this or am already perfect; but I press on to make it my own, because Christ Jesus has made me his own. Brethren, I do not consider that I have made it my own; but one thing I do, forgetting what lies behind and straining forward to what lies ahead, I press on toward the goal for the prize of the upward call of God in Christ Jesus (Philippians 3:12-14 RSV).

If we, like Paul, place our confidence in God and do our best to conform our lives to his will, we can be as sure that we will be victorious: "I know whom I have believed, and am persuaded that he is able to keep that which I have committed unto him against that day" (2 Timothy 1:12b KJ). Paul *knew* his Heavenly Father; he trusted him to keep his promises. Through the scriptures we *know* God and *can know* we are walking in the light.

B. The wise woman realizes that her spiritual success depends on individual performance. Just as an athlete can not win his athletic letter because other members of the team performed well, we can not expect to go to heaven because the congregation where we worship has good leadership and an effective program. Of course an athlete may be spurred to better performance by action of his coaches and team mates. We surely will grow spiritually by involvement with a spiritually effective congregation. But in the final analysis, we will be judged individually, "For we must all appear before the judgment seat of Christ; that every one may receive the things done in his body, according to that he hath done, whether it be good or bad" (2 Corinthians 5:10 KJ). The wise woman is careful to sow to the Spirit; the foolish sows to the flesh; God's records are accurate; they are current, only those sins not removed by the blood of Christ will be faced at judgment:

> Do not be deceived; God is not mocked, for whatever a man sows, that he will also reap. For he who sows to his own flesh will from the flesh reap corruption; but he who sows to the Spirit will from the Spirit reap eternal life. And let us not grow weary in well-doing, for in due season we shall reap, if we do not lose heart (Galatians 6:7-10 RSV).

C. Because of her diligence in the Christian race, the wise woman looks forward to an abundant entrance into God's eternal kingdom. Through her knowledge of Jesus Christ, she has been supplied with everything she needs for living the truly good life. Accepting his wonderful promises, she has been able to escape the grasp of her carnal nature, the disintegration that lust produces in the world, and has become a partaker of the divine nature, growing in Christian graces and abounding in spiritual fruit:

> His divine power has granted to us all things that pertain to life and godliness, through the knowledge of him who called us to his own glory and excellence, by which he has granted to us his precious and very great promises, that through these you may escape from the corruption that is in the world because of passion, and become partakers of the divine nature. For this very reason make every effort to supplement your faith with virtue, and virtue with knowledge, and knowledge with self-control, and self-control with steadfastness, and steadfastness with godliness, and godliness with brotherly affection, and brotherly affection with love. For if these things are yours and abound, they keep you from being ineffective or unfruitful in the knowledge of our Lord Jesus Christ. For whoever lacks these things is blind and shortsighted and has forgotten that he was cleansed from his old sins. Therefore, brethren, be more

zealous to confirm your call and election, for if you do this you will never fail; so there will be richly provided for you an entrance into the eternal kingdom of our Lord and Savior Jesus Christ (2 Peter 1:3-11 RSV).

IV. THEN SHALL WE APPEAR WITH HIM IN GLORY. Her sinful life having died with Christ, who then is her life, the wise woman looks forward joyfully to his coming again; she has been promised that she then will be manifested with him in glory. Like the heroes of faith extolled in Hebrews 11, she has had her eyes fixed on her true homeland, heaven, while she traveled homeward as an exile or stranger on the earth. With them, she desires a better country, a heavenly one, "Therefore God is not ashamed to be called their God, for he has prepared for them a city" (Hebrews 11:13-17 RSV).

A. The beauty of the heavenly city is beyond human ability to describe; even inspired writers describe it in symbols to give us just a hint of its true grandeur. It is perfection, for God, himself, is its architect and builder (Hebrews 11:10). Our only eye witness description of heaven was penned by John, who was given a special revelation to transmit to us so that we might be encouraged as we travel toward that city which can be described only by inspiration:

> I saw the Holy City, the new Jerusalem, coming down out of heaven from God, prepared as a bride beautifully dressed for her husband...One of the seven angels who had the seven bowls full of seven last plagues came and said to me, "Come, I will show you the bride, the wife of the Lamb." And he carried me away in the Spirit to a mountain great and high, and showed me the Holy City, Jerusalem, coming down out of heaven from God. It shone with the glory of God, and its brilliance was like that of a very precious jewel, like a jasper, clear as crystal...The wall was made of jasper and the city of pure gold, as pure as glass...The twelve gates were twelve pearls, each gate made of a single pearl. The street of the city was of pure gold, like transparent glass. I did not see a temple in the city, because the Lord God Almighty and the Lamb are its temple. The city does not need the sun or the moon to shine on it, for the glory of God gives it light, and the Lamb is its lamp...On no day will its gates ever be shut, for there will be no night there (Revelations 21:2; 9-12a; 18; 21-23; 25 NIV).

B. Jesus will welcome us to mansions in the sky. As he was being stoned to death, Stephen, the first to die for proclaiming Christ, was given a glimpse into heaven. We are told he looked up to heaven and saw the glory of God, and Jesus standing at the right hand of God (Acts 7:55). Near the close of his earthly ministry, Jesus had warned the apostles that he would be going back to the Father. He assured them, though, that he would be waiting there for them (and us): "In my Father's house are many rooms; if it were not so, I would have told you. I am going there to prepare a place for you. And if I go and prepare a place for you, I will come back and take you to be with me that you also may be where I am" (John 14:2-3 NIV).

Because of her life in Christ, the wise woman will claim her room (mansion, KJ) in heaven.

C. Her heavenly home will be well furnished, for she will be able to claim the treasures she has laid up there. Remember, Jesus said, "Do not lay up for yourselves treasures on earth, where moth and rust consume and where thieves break in and steal, but lay up for yourselves treasures in heaven, where neither moth nor rust consumes and where thieves do not break in and steal. For where your treasure is, there will your heart be also" (Matthew 6:19-21 RSV).

Because her heart has been set on earthly things, the foolish woman will find no treasures laid up for her in heaven. Yes, she will collect her wages..."For the wages of sin is death" (Romans 6:23a).

The wise woman's heart has been set on things above; ample treasures are awaiting her arrival!

D. She will be well dressed as she mingles with the saints. She made preparation during her sojourn on earth. She paid heed to the admonition to "fling off the dirty clothes of the old way of living, which were rotted through and through with lust's illusions, and, with yourselves mentally and spiritually remade, to put on the clean fresh clothes of the new life which was made by God's design for righteousness and holiness which is no illusion" (Ephesians 4:22-24 P). She wears designer clothes! They are snowy white, for they were washed in the blood of the Lamb. Thus clothed, she is among the blessed who have a right to the tree of life:

> Blessed are those who wash their robes, that they may have the right to the tree of life and may go through the gates into the city. Outside are the dogs, those who practice magic arts, the sexually immoral, the murderers, the idolaters and everyone who loves and practices falsehood (Revelation 22:14-15 NIV).

How sad that those who may be good by the world's standards will be in the vile company outside the gates because they failed to obey- -to wash their clothes in the blood of the lamb, that is, to be baptized into Christ.

Completing the wise woman's costume will be the crown of righteousness, "which the Lord, the righteous Judge, will award" (2 Timothy 4:8).

E. She will mingle in heavenly fellowship. She will join the angels in praising her Lord, Jesus, and the Heavenly Father. John gives a truly inspiring picture of this fellowship:

> And after this I looked and there before me was a great multitude that no one could count, from every nation, tribe, people and language, standing before the throne and in front of the Lamb. They were wearing white robes and were holding palm branches in their hands. And they cried out in a loud voice:
>
> "Salvation belongs to our God,
> who sits on the throne,
> and to the Lamb."
>
> All the angels were standing around the throne and around the elders and the four living creatures. They fell down on their faces before the throne and worshiped God, saying:
>
> "Amen!
> Praise and glory
> and wisdom and thanks and honor
> and power and strength
> be to our God for ever and ever.
> Amen!" (Revelation 7:9-12 NIV).

F. Like the Fairy Princess, the wise woman will live happily ever after. Perhaps among the throngs from every nation she will find her mother and father, brothers, and sisters, sons and daughters, and hosts of brothers and sisters in Christ with whom she shared the journey to heaven. There can be no note of sadness, for she is with the Father and Son, joining in their everlasting praise. John was told, "God himself will be with them and be their God. He will wipe every tear from their eyes. There will be no more death or mourning or crying or pain, for the old order of things has passed away" (Revelation 21:3-4 NIV). Her happy voice will mingle with "what sounded like a great multitude, like the roar of rushing waters and like loud peals of thunder, shouting:

"Hallelujah!
For our Lord God Almighty reigns.
Let us rejoice and be glad and give him glory!
For the wedding of the lamb has come
and his bride has made herself ready."
(Revelation 19:6-7 NIV).

CONCLUSION: The foolish woman will have heard her sentence, "Depart from me; I never knew you." The wise woman will have reached her glorious destination.

DAILY BIBLE READINGS:
Sunday: Galatians 5:19-24, flesh or Spirit
Monday: Hebrews 4:1-16, confidence, in Christ
Tuesday: 2 Corinthians 9:1-15, abundant provisions
Wednesday: 2 Timothy 3:1-17, Shun evil; be equipped for good.
Thursday: 1 Corinthians 15:35-58, mortality, immortality
Friday: 2 Peter 1:3-11, Make your election sure.
Saturday: Revelation 21:1-27, home of the soul
MEMORY VERSES:
Colossians 3:1-4

EPILOGUE

My prayer is that this study has lead you to a deeper appreciation of God's word and of the importance in your own life of a knowledge of the scriptures.

May you have grown in your knowledge of God, Christ, and the Holy Spirit--may you really KNOW them as indispensable companions in your daily life.

May you realize that it is only in Christ you will be able to leave behind your old self, which may have been full of doubt, degredation, and defeat, and become a new person, knowing true freedom, happiness, peace, and contentment.

May you walk confidently in THE WAY, enjoying the fellowship of the saints and looking forward with joy to your destination: everlasting life in that eternal city where God is the light, where there will be no sorrow or separation, where we shall always be with the Lord.

In the words of Paul, "May you be filled with the knowledge of his will in all spiritual wisdom and understanding, to lead a life worthy of the Lord, fully pleasing to him, bearing fruit in every good work and increasing in the knowledge of God" (Colossians 1:9b-10 RSV).

--Bessie Patterson

BIBLIOGRAPHY

A. D. Adams, *Cruden's Complete Concordance*, et al, eds., C. E. I. Publishing Co., Box 858, Athens, Ala. 1949

Foster, Mrs. Montie McGinty, *A Higher Plane*, Fidelity Book & Supply, P.O. Box 1739, Abilene, TX, 1968.

Halley, Henry H., *Bible Handbook*, Henry H. Halley, Box 774, Chicago 90, Ill., 1959.

Peloubert, F. N., *Peloubert's Bible Dictionary*, The John C. Winston Company, Philadelphia, Chicago, 1925.

Thompson's *The New Chain Reference Bible*, Kirkbride Bible Co., Indianapolis, Indiana, U. S. A. 1929.

Tolle, James M., *The Christian Graces*, Tolle Publications, Box 13, Fullerton, Calf 92632, 1965.

Vine, W. E., *An Expository Dictionary of New Testament Words*, Fleming H. Revell Co., Old Tappan, New Jersey, 1966.

Williams, Leewin B., *Encyclopedia of Wit Humor and Wisdom*, Abingdon-Cokesbury Press, New York, Nashville, 1949.

Woods, Guy N., *New Testament Commentaries, Peter, John, Jude*, Gospel Advocate Co., Nashville, Tenn., 1953.